BRANCHES TO HEAVEN

BRANCHES
TO HEAVEN

The Geniuses of C. S. Lewis

JAMES COMO

SPENCE PUBLISHING COMPANY · DALLAS
1998

Published in the United States by
Spence Publishing Company
111 Cole Street
Dallas, Texas 75207

Library of Congress Cataloging-in-Publication Data
for the Hardcover Edition

Como, James T.
    Branches to heaven : the geniuses of C. S. Lewis / James Como
        p. cm.
    Includes bibliographical references and index.
    ISBN 1-890626-01-5 (hardcover)
    1. Lewis, C. S. (Clive Staples), 1898-1963—Criticism and
interpretation.   2. Lewis, C. S. (Clive Staples), 1898-1963—
Knowledge and learning.   3. Christian literature, English—
History and criticism.   4. Fantastic fiction, English—History
and criticism.   I. Title.
PR6023.E926Z6413   1998
823'.912—dc21   98-24612

ISBN 1-890626-15-5 (pbk.)

Printed in the United States of America

To our parents,

Helen and Joseph,

In Memoriam.

Over this your white grave
the flowers of life in white—
so many years without you—
how many have passed out of sight?

Over this your white grave
covered for years, there is a stir
in the air, something uplifting
and, like death, beyond comprehension.

Over this your white grave
oh, mother [and father], can such loving cease
for all [our] filial adoration
a prayer:
Give [them] eternal peace—

—Karol Wojtyla

Contents

Preface   ix

Introduction: Genius   3

PART I

ROOTS

1   Will   23

2   Grammar   55

3   Spirit   83

PART II

BRANCHES

4   Word   111

5   Rhetoric   139

6   Rhetorica Religii   167

Epilogue: Silence   195

A Brief Chronology   201

Works Consulted   205

Index   217

Preface

C. S. LEWIS IS THE SORT OF AUTHOR—a "discovery" of the first order—that compels a reader to spread the word, so strikingly direct and familiar is his voice, so bracing his thought. You might have begun with what I call the "you, too?" reflex, "you, too?" being what you whispered with happy surprise three decades ago when you noticed someone else engrossed in a Lewis tome. You go on to gather fellow enthusiasts into a society dedicated to the study and enjoyment of his work. But because you do not want anyone to miss out on even the smallest morsel of him, and because you think you understand those morsels so well, after a while you presume to make the already-pellucidly-clear clearer still. Before you know it, you are writing, teaching, and lecturing about him. There are other authors, of course, who matter to you—some greater than he and many of very telling importance. But he abides, dwelling within and designing much of your own internal landscape.

Though greatly esteemed, Lewis is, one hundred years after his birth and thirty-five after his death, under- and wrongly-estimated. Because of his anti-modern stance as a self-styled "dinosaur," his staggering accessibility, the attempt by some readers to draft him into a movement, and to an effort by some commentators to lay an almost gnostic claim on his legacy, Lewis seems somehow intellectually and artistically marginal. Furthermore, in studies of his work, the breadth of his learning, the distinctiveness and acuity of his thinking, and the scope of his intellectual and literary reach are routinely assumed, but unexamined as such.

Possessed of a highly nuanced, as well as an astonishingly well-furnished intellect, a religious faith devoid of anything remotely facile, rhetorical gifts arguably unmatched in this century in their adroitness and versatility, inexhaustible powers of invention, and a will to deploy all of these, C. S. Lewis is a far more complex and sophisticated figure than the ease of his style and the popularity of his work suggest. The contours of his current reputation give scant sign of the rootedness and richness of his achievements: He is among the great men of letters in the English-speaking world, not only in this century but ever; he is one of the most nourishing, relevant, and effective religious thinkers of this century; and within the ambit of Lewis's prevailing genius were several other geniuses of considerable moment and magnitude.

Except briefly in the Introduction, I barely defend these claims. I posit them early, not because they have been forcefully defended by anyone, but because they have been forcefully stated by no one. I merely ask readers to regard them as plausible. They indicate my interests and therefore partially explain my "enthusiasm"; but they are not premises and need not be granted, even for the sake of my argument. I know that many, even many devoted, studious, and very learned, readers of Lewis disagree with them. But these are my settled critical opinions, and I trust they do not compromise my judgment.

"The true genius," wrote Dr. Johnson in his *Life of Cowley*, "is a mind of large general powers accidentally determined to some particular direction." And Bulwer-Lytton sharpens the point with "genius does what it must, talent what it can." But an older sense of *genius* persists, one which Lewis knew well, commented upon, and used in his fiction, that of a "tutelary spirit." This sense of the word is not uncommon, as when we say a person has "a genius" for, say, self-promotion, or for saying just the right thing, or for choosing the right combination of colors when dressing. It is this sense of genius that I intend when claiming that Lewis had several of them, which is among the reasons he is so frequently misconstrued. I would seek out those several geniuses and explore the landscape about which they played.

Of course, Lewis would not countenance such a search and, his so-called "personal heresy" aside, he would object for a most interesting reason. "My own secret is," he wrote to his brother in June of 1932, "*I don't like genius.* I like enormously some *things* that only genius can do. . . . What I don't care twopence about is the sense (apparently dear to so many) of being in the hands of 'a great man'—you know, his dazzling personality, his lightening energy, the strange force of his mind—and all that." Now by "genius" I do indeed mean precisely "all that," for the "great man" Lewis has described is himself. But I mean still more. Near the beginning of his wonderful autobiography, *The Golden String*, Dom Bede Griffiths writes that people "will not be converted by words or arguments, for God . . . is the very ground of existence. We have to encounter him as a fact of our existence before we can really be persuaded to believe in him. To discover God is not to discover an idea but to discover oneself. It is to awake to that part of one's existence which has been hidden from sight and which one has refused to recognize." He concludes that "the discovery may be very painful; it is like going through a kind of death. But it is the one thing that makes life worth living." Now, the chronology of Lewis's life and its major motifs are well-established—or so it seems. I argue that much of what he revealed about himself was "apologetic," revelations of choices made from hard-won knowledge of himself, which could not—not even with Lewis—be all the knowledge there was to be had. So by "genius" I mean especially Lewis's "inner landscape," with respect to which he was so coy and evasive, but from which the dazzle emerges. In short, I mean the roots of his vocation and the branches of his rhetorical and personal achievements.

If this were the eighteenth century, when authors routinely employed long, descriptive, and therefore useful subtitles, mine would be something like "an enquiry into the sort of writer Lewis was above all, the kind of work he produced and whence he produced it, followed by a prescription for how best to apprehend him, assess his achievement, and appreciate his labor; with emphasis upon the theory, tradition, and application of Rhetoric and of its several parts and upon the difficulties, mostly spiritual, which its practice effected." But such a title would not be very much shorter than this short book, in which I hope to bring into coherent shape a number of ideas about C. S. Lewis and his work that have lingered with me over the past thirty-five years.

Though in and of themselves some of these ideas are old and a bit worn, others are old but not worn at all, while still others are new and deserve some discussion. Nevertheless, if there be freshness in this effort it must lie more in its overall view of Lewis, and how we come by it than in any individual claim. My audience, I think, is the generally literate reader who has heard about Lewis, who has read some of Lewis and would read more, and who is both curious and industrious. In its major aspect *Branches to Heaven* is a preface. There are few new facts, and hardly any material new to the experienced student of Lewis, but my view of newness, not unlike Lewis's of "originality," is that it is much overrated. (Walter Hooper's magisterial *Companion and Guide*, for example, does not pretend to newness or to critical ingenuity, though along the way it provides them; but its synthesizing and scholarly power makes for unrelenting freshness.) On the other hand, *Branches to Heaven* is no general introduction, and I do hope that those who have read much of Lewis will find in the pages that follow something of interest, if not to accept then to argue with, and if not that then at least to ponder. As I develop my reflections, I hope they will reveal a Lewis genius of great, very particular, and most subtle and demanding order.

HAPPILY DO I THANK the authors and experts (my debts are obvious), especially in England and at Wheaton College; the colleagues, students, and audiences, especially at York College in Jamaica, Queens, and at the Fifth Avenue Presbyterian Church in Manhattan; and the friends, supporters, and fellow pilgrims, especially of the New York C. S. Lewis Society, who variously have taught us all much about CSL over the past few decades, have built a reliable body of knowledge about him, and who have indulged my personal interest to an inexplicably high degree.

Particularly I thank Clara Sarrocco and Bob Merchant of the New York C. S. Lewis Society; Forbes Hill, the unself-conscious mentor who taught me much more than most of the rhetoric I know; and former students and dear friends Timothy Corkery (whose insight into Lewis as an existential writer has proved especially valuable) and the late Anthony W. Marotta Jr., who was always a revelrous inspiration to hard thinking and even harder work and to ever greater goodness. Grateful prayer for the joyous homecoming of his soul, and for the souls of C. S., W. H., Flora, and Albert Lewis, is never out of season.

My family here on earth would prefer I not thank them in print, but that is too bad: husbands and fathers have certain prerogatives. So I thank young Jim, Helen Alexandra, and my good wife Alejandra, *la sposa di tutte le spose*. This book is dedicated to my family in Heaven.

BRANCHES TO HEAVEN

Genius

P ERHAPS BECAUSE two hundred years of Enlightenment rationalism have gotten us down, we in the West have sought out a New Age, marked by the ludicrous prophecies of one Celestine and the proliferation of 1-900 psychic hotline numbers. All the while we harbor what Wayne Booth has called the *sub*stitious disbelief in anything that we either have not invented or does not make us *feel*, feel *comfortable*, and feel comfortable *with ourselves*. In short, we lurch towards that of which we deny the possibility, objective truth, the abolition of which has given rise to radical subjectivism as a response to its predecessor, nineteenth-century determinism. Even if the stars and planets, your infantile sexuality, history, society, and genes (or even jeans) made you what you are, and you are not as logically positive as once you were, well, then you may construct an alternative you, an alternative reality, fresh truths—indeed, whole new belief systems.

All this has been going on long enough finally to have been named: *postmodern*. This, our zeitgeist, is marked by a new "belief about belief," as Walter Truett Anderson has written. Stephen Toulmin puts it this way:

3

> We must reconcile ourselves to a paradoxical-sounding
> thought: namely, the thought that *we no longer live in
> the "modern world"* .... Our own natural science today
> is no longer "modern" science: Instead ... it is rapidly
> engaged in becoming "postmodern" science: the science
> of the "post-modern" world, of "post-nationalist" poli-
> tics, and "post-industrial" society—the world that has not
> yet discovered how to define itself in terms of what it *is*,
> but only in terms of what it has *just now ceased to be*.

What *is* new, then, is the intellectual context in which this
radical subjectivism occurs: there is none, that is, no single
one. Well, since without context nothing has a fixed or reliable meaning, whatever-it-is-we-are-now floats in a void,
untethered, at once bloated and gushing, calamitously unre-
strained, seemingly buoyant, but in fact naive about the depth
of its own despair.

This new void does not result from the absence of old-
time religious practice, nor of religious *feeling*. We are not
surprised when the Episcopal journal *Mission and Ministry*
issues a special anthology number (volume XI, number 1) entitled "Reading for Renewal." But neither can we be surprised
when the *New York Times Magazine* publishes a special issue
on "God Decentralized" (December 7, 1997) and does not sneer;
or when the magazine *Self* (yes, *Self*!) in December 1997 publishes a "special inspirational issue" subtitled "Your Spiritual
Life," and means it—nearly 80 percent of us pray at least once
a week, nearly 60 percent daily. Rather, the void results from
the absence, and denigration, of that which is fundamentally
designed to reconstitute meaning in the first place: serious
religious thinking.

As the wave of postmodernism rises to its crest, given even
more force by the approach of a millennium, its successor can

be seen on the horizon, preceded by calls for the re-introduc-
tion of religion into the public square. And even now, arguably one of the greatest religious and literary geniuses of the
century remains poised to answer the call. On the eve of the
centenary of his birth, C. S. Lewis is, as he has been for nearly
seventy years, the provident voice. It was sixty years ago that
he diagnosed our age as "post-Christian," and fifty that he
warned us about the "Poison of Subjectivism." He predicted
a strength so hideous that Value itself would fall before it,
allowing the most horrific re-inventions that would lead, not
only to the "abolition of man," but to a reign of Nonsense, a
deconstructed world of relativism, selfism, and unbelief in
which "everything has been seen through," even man himself—
a world so transparent as to be invisible.

I

Neither the *Times Magazine* nor *Self* mentioned C. S. Lewis
at all or, for that matter, any canonical spiritual writer of great
note. But this prophet and diagnostician also gives the prescription. The only reason to believe anything, Lewis maintained, is because that thing is true. And this axiom he turned
upon religious belief, from *a priori* questions, such as Is reason valid? and By way of it do we gain access to the *Tao*, or
natural law?, to the probability of a concrete supernatural and
visions of a grand design; from questions about prayer, the
various genres of scripture, and the possibility of miracles, to
the psychology of temptation, the dilemma of the unarrived
Second Coming, and the "transposition" of nature. As fabulist, romancer, novelist, allegorist, poet, essayist, preacher,
broadcaster (his was the second most-recognized voice after
Churchill's during World War II), public lecturer and debater,

conversationalist, and letter-writer, Lewis was indefatigable—no challenge too great or, as important, too small, no audience too unlearned or remote. Lewis possessed one of the most formidable minds of the century: "He reads everything and remembers everything he's read," said William Empson, more literally accurate than he could know. As literary historian, theorist, critic, and reviewer, his brilliance, wit, authority, and clarity make him still the standard against which others in his field are measured and against which those who would take him on are matched.

Lewis never exhorted or even argued directly in support of a single religious tenet, but rather marshaled great learning with seeming effortlessness in order to clear away obstacles to belief, to make questions accessible to reason, and finally, in virtually all that he wrote, to remind us that we, here, are but sojourners. Whether it be logical positivism, psychological or historical determinism, the Enlightenment, or postmodernist fads and fancies, "anything not eternal," he insisted, "is eternally out of date."

The antidote, then, to our self-delusional new "belief about belief" is a restoration. Patrick Glyn, in his provocative *God: The Evidence*, describes and vindicates the "anthropic principle," achieving a "reconciliation of Faith and Reason in a Postsecular World," thus catching up with Lewis, who has been waiting all along. His appeal has grown with the want of meaning in our lives, even as his reputation has been mown for a "major motion picture," a *Love Story*, yet, for the 1990s. To see Lewis at once within a great tradition of religious thought and as its embodiment, to see him as a member of many different constellations of writers—MacDonald, Chesterton, and Lewis; Undset, Wilder, Percy, and Lewis; Swift, Johnson, and Lewis; Hooker, Baxter, Bunyan, Law, and Lewis—would be to restore context, arresting much of our intellectual drift on the one hand, and reclaiming some fixed hope on the other. After all, as Dr. Johnson said, "people need to be reminded more often than instructed."

II

Altogether Lewis published some forty books; in addition, he saw to print over two hundred short pieces and nearly eighty poems, excluding those in the cycle *Spirits in Bondage* or included as parts of longer works. Consider the array of the essays alone: critical, historical, and theoretical work on literature; religious (analytical, inquisitive, conceptual, and polemical); philosophical; and finally social and cultural commentary. And since his death many more books have come forth, previously unpublished works or collections of otherwise scattered pieces, including letters and a diary.

We must remember that there is one Lewis in many modes; and although different audiences may know of the various incarnations, they do not necessarily have a direct acquaintance with each of them. Most who read *Mere Christianity* did not hear the BBC broadcasts from which it is taken. Lewis's current reputation rests upon familiarity with the book; his original reputation was largely made by the broadcasts. They are separate reputations, with a hearsay knowledge of the earlier assisting the later. Among Lewis's greatest nonfiction works are a handful of his sermons: moving, significant, illuminating. They are regarded as famous even by those who did not hear them; they are even regarded as famous by those who have not read them, for the slim volumes in which they are collected are not widely known, let alone widely purchased. *The Screwtape Letters* was an immediate success and remains one of Lewis's most popular books; but *Screwtape* came out, first in serial form, then almost immediately as a book, during the war when Lewis was at the height of his Space-trilogy and, especially, B B C-broadcast fame. His reputation then was not, as rhetoricians say, a prior reputation but a current one, with great cumulative power.

Lewis, like some nations, forged a number of "spheres of influence" which vary over time and among different audiences. Devoted readers of the *Chronicles of Narnia* may not have read, or even know of, *The Screwtape Letters*, surely his second-best-known work and the one which got his picture on the cover of *Time* in 1947. The scholar is likely unknown to the readers of the Space trilogy. Those who know well *Mere Christianity* may not have read either the subtle *Problem of Pain* or the short analytical essays or the sermons. Still fewer will have read Lewis's lyrical poetry; and almost no one even knows of his long narrative poems.

So whole generations have "discovered" this or that part of Lewis as though it were the *only* part. But enough people have discovered enough parts for Lewis to be a recognizable reference in the works of others. Robertson Davies and Tom Wolfe could drop his name in their novels secure in the knowledge that audiences would know whom they meant and why they were dropping it; Walker Percy could use one of his most prominent ideas, *Sehnsucht* (or Joy), as coin of the realm; and he could be referred to, or quoted by, the likes of Pope John Paul II, Margaret Thatcher, Ronald Reagan, and George Bush ("a thousand points of light" is from *The Magician's Nephew*, the first of the seven *Chronicles of Narnia*). Aspects of Lewis's life and work unknown and virtually unknowable two decades ago have become common knowledge. Finally, Lewis's sociocultural epiphany was official: Hollywood exploited him in

Shadowlands. All along, though, he has been and remains the same Jack, as Lewis was known to his friends.

As I write, there are four Lewis anthologies, one encyclopedic; two indexes, one general and the other to words in his poetry; two sequential annotated checklists to shelves-full of secondary sources; one handbook, with another forthcoming; a companion to *Narnia*; an anthology of commentary and reviews; four major biographies; and Walter Hooper's *Companion and Guide.* Most of his titles are in print, those that are not are easily obtained, and many of them are very widely translated. Societies, institutes, and foundations devoted to the study and perpetuation of his work now abound worldwide. He is frequently visited in cyberspace, and soon his fully-restored Oxford home will be open to visitors in actual space. There are three major university repositories of work by, or related to, him. Tours are conducted of Lewis sites, memorial statues and stones are being carved, a centenary office has been established, and a commemorative stamp has been issued. Even the Vicar of Holy Trinity parish, Lewis's church in Headington Quarry, has noticed. Some years ago Fr. Christopher Hewetson wrote to his congregation that he "thinks [they] are forced to improve [their] connection with C. S. Lewis." He continues, "When I came here three and a half years ago. . . . [t]here was a certain 'yes but'. I found it difficult to get a well known preacher to preach at the dedication of the Narnia window. Since then his rating has increased. . . . He was a very committed Christian, a man of great prayer. . . . We must be proud of our connection with him and learn from it. Ideas here would be welcome."

Lewis's popularity has gone through many metamorphoses, from a very great height in the 1930s, 1940s, and 1950s as a literary scholar, to another, quite separate towering peak in

the 1940s and 1950s as an apologist, to a waning of both shortly
before his death, and then to obscurity shortly thereafter. The
slow re-ascent began, I think, in the mid-1970s, some dozen
years after his death, as more of his work appeared and several Lewis societies took hold. At this time, academic interest began to take hold as well and a veritable Lewis industry
was established. (In the late 1970s, an editor from Eerdmans,
long one of Lewis's publishers, was heard to cry at a convention of the Modern Language Association, "no more books on
Lewis, please!") A plateau was then reached, as many Lewis
titles, and the contents of titles, were juggled about, sometimes
between publishers.

Really what we are discussing is the sociology of reputation, no simple matter after all. Once a reputation has reified
into celebrity it assumes a life of its own. Now, a celebrity is
a person, according to Daniel Boorstin, "who is famous for
being well-known." That celebrity has descended upon Lewis
is beyond dispute, as evidenced by Richard Attenborough's
woefully-simplistic-yet-soppily-effective *Shadowlands*. Yet even
much earlier than 1995 the syndrome had struck Lewis. On
the one hand, he had been denied the larger reputation which
his work so clearly warrants, being widely regarded—or more
likely, dismissed—as a "lay theologian" or "popularizer"; on
the other, his devoted and growing readership scarcely knows
him as a scholar, critic, reviewer, social commentator, philosopher, poet, *and* elegant essayist.

To the questions, Whence C. S. Lewis's appeal? and Why
does it endure?, my answer commonly has itself been a question along the lines of, How much of him have you read? It
is an impatient answer, and an unreasonable one, I have come
to see, since so many otherwise well-read and even-tempered
people continue to ask these questions. So here, again, is the

short answer: C. S. Lewis is among the greatest men of letters of the twentieth century. Not only was he a writer of enormous genius, but he was possessed of very many *geniuses*, lending him a versatility and scope of achievement virtually unparalleled in this tide of times. The claim wants vindication, of course, in an examination of those geniuses. This is no easy task, for that claim, which I had once regarded as obvious, turns out to have much greater depth and complexity than meets even the favorably predisposed eye. In other words, it was not so obvious to begin with; rather, it is intuitively accessible.

Consider again, for a moment, those constellations of literary practice within which Lewis might rightly be placed. He was a children's fabulist, *The Chronicles of Narnia* proving sufficiently popular and artistically provocative to merit comparison with Lewis Carroll's *Alice* books. His literary history and criticism make him the standard by which such giants as William Empson, Douglas Bush, E. M. W. Tillyard, and the unlikely aspirant to Lewis's style and stance, Stanley Fish, must be judged. As a cultural critic writing on religion he anticipated the likes of Richard John Neuhaus, Stephen Carter, and Harold Bloom, all of whom have discovered what Lewis knew sixty-five years ago when he called ours a post-Christian age: Our naked public square needs missionaries as much as old China. As a literary journalist and social critic he might have, had he produced more in these genres, kept company with the likes of Edmund Wilson or Dwight MacDonald. His speculative fictions have earned him the admiration of fantasy readers and practitioners alike, for example, Madeleine L'Engle and Brian Aldiss. The satires, especially *The Screwtape Letters*, are simply masterworks, in the same league as the satires of the eighteenth-century giants; and his one real novel, *Till We Have*

Faces, is his masterpiece, a classic, and typically unnoticed, post-Jamesian psychological study that puts him in the company of the rarest literary lights of this century.

Even without his consistently fine, often brilliant, and sometimes soaring, but withal minor, poetry, and without his philosophical work there should be enough genius—enough geniuses—to satisfy anyone. But why omit the philosophy? His defense of natural law, *The Abolition of Man*, is a landmark, weakened by its brevity, I think, but nonetheless seminal. I have not yet mentioned his letters, which will fill three volumes, conversation which has been compared to Dr. Johnson's, and his careers as a public speaker—preacher, debater, and broadcaster. And for all of his adult life he was a teacher, as a tutor no Mr. Chips, to be sure, but as a lecturer without equal. Is it any wonder that an innocent inquiry into the sources of his appeal and of its longevity should provoke impatience? And yet—amazingly—the array of work constitutes only a fraction of the answer, for its says nothing of the writing *per se* of Lewis or of his thought and voice. Perhaps he makes it all look too easy, fluent, and angst-free.

III

This mere array of work says nothing of Lewis's most important genius, antecedent to most of the others and warranting his willed commitment to an apologetic vocation. As an apologist, of course, he is in the company of both G. K. Chesterton and George MacDonald. Not too long ago, certainly within the lifetime of a good number of readers of this book, well-muscled Christian apologetics was a thriving enterprise, as Chesterton, Dorothy L. Sayers, Frank Sheed, J. B. Phillips, Arnold Lunn, Fulton Sheen, and many others held the field.

But it seems to have fallen out of favor. "Apologetic," meaning "defense," has come to mean saying "sorry." Austin Farrer, a dear friend of Lewis's and a formidable apologist-theologian, thought that a flourishing apologetic indicated a faith under strong attack. This is undoubtedly true, but the converse is not. A dramatically diminished apologetic does not mean a faith secure from assault: it may have been relegated to the basement. Expressions of religious faith, like most other expressions, are subject to trends; and since the 1930s, when Lewis began his apologetic career, we have had our share.

Now we seem to be in that age of "feeling good" about ourselves and others. But if faith is feeling, as opposed to belief, what is there to defend? One indeed says "sorry" more than "you are wrong," which is so unattractively judgmental, and apologetic becomes apologizing. In short, religious, and not just Christian, apologetics has declined, not because faith is no longer under attack, but because its claims to truth seem increasingly irrelevant in an Age of Emotion, when "enhanced personality," "wellness," and "personal integration" matter more than, and exist apart from, sound, rigorously-tested, fully-informed belief. It is an aspect of Lewis's apologetic genius that he discerned and understood this problem better than anyone before or since. He noted that we post-Christians are to pagans what divorcees are to virgins. We are no longer wedded to our spiritual convictions, since "conviction"—intellectual apprehension and commitment—seems to matter so little to begin with. Why does this trivializing of conviction matter so much? Lewis provides the answer, and it is among the most important things he ever wrote, self-evident but not therefore obvious, and worthy of repetition. The only reason to believe in Christianity—not one faith among many, but the only one—is the same reason for believing in anything: it is true. Not that it makes us feel good, or even "well"; not that "it works for us"; not even that we are "comfortable" with it; but that it is, simply, true. If one does not think a thing true, then why believe it at all? Indeed, what could "believe" mean in such a case?

The faith is timeless: its interpreters might make it fresh, but not original. This is precisely the distinction Lewis saw in his own apologetic models, people such as St. Athanasius and William Law. And not only does the faith not change, but we live in "enemy-occupied territory." The heresies merely seem new, but they never are—except for the heresy that there can be no heresies, thus the "post" in post-Christian. They are, though, unceasing. This is why Lewis was, in one sense, relentlessly militant, a "frontiersman," as Austin Farrer described him: "There are frontiersmen and frontiersmen, of course. There is what one might call the Munich school, who will always sell the pass. . . . They are too busy learning from their enemies to do much in defense of their friends. The typical apologist is a man whose every dyke is his last ditch. He will carry the war into the enemy's own country; he will not yield an inch of his own."

One of the most potent and dangerous heresies was that of Arius during the reign of Constantine in the fourth century. Arius denied the divinity of Christ, holding (as Jehovah's Witnesses now do) that he was not of one substance with God but merely the highest of created beings. But for one man, St. Athanasius (ca. 297-373), Arianism would have triumphed. He lived, wrote, suffered, and finally prevailed, securing for all Christians the Nicene Creed. Lewis knew Athanasius's work well and, I think, borrowed from it. In his introduction to a translation of St. Athanasius's *On the Incarnation*, Lewis notes that the Saint resisted "one of those 'sensible' synthetic religions which are so rigorously recommended today and which, then as now, included among their devotees many highly cultivated clergymen. It is his glory that he did not move with the times; it is his reward that he now remains when those times, as all times do, have moved away."

That is why Lewis championed "Mere Christianity," a phrase he adopted from Richard Baxter (1615-91), a Nonconformist clergyman who was persecuted when he left the Church of England. No "insipid interdenominational transparency," this Mere Christianity is the same set of convictions that St. Athanasius would profess. Lewis recalled "In the days when I still hated Christianity, I learned to recognize, like some all too familiar smell, that almost unvarying *something* which met me, now in Puritan Bunyan, now in Anglican Hooker, now in Thomist Dante. It was there (honeyed and floral) in François de Sales; . . . it was there (grim but manful) in Pascal and Johnson. . . . It was, of course, varied; and yet . . . not to be evaded, the odour which is death to us until we allow it to become life. . . . ," that is, something worth defending and not be sorry over: orthodox Christianity. As is true of almost every other idea Lewis propounded, this one is old, at least as old as the apologetic tradition itself, starting with the Apostles, especially St. Paul. Lewis certainly saw himself as firmly within that tradition. In a paper entitled "Christian Apologetics" Lewis defined "Mere Christianity": "[T]he faith preached by the Apostles, attested by the martyrs, embodied in the Creeds, expounded by the Fathers. . . . Each of us has his individual emphasis: each holds, in addition to the Faith, many opinions which seem to him to be consistent with it and true and important. And so perhaps they are. But as apologists it is not our business to defend *them*. We are defending Christianity; not 'my religion'."

IV

How might we judge Lewis and his world of words (we shall see that the two are really one)? In his unpretentious, prescient, and penetrating work of literary theory, *An Experiment in Criticism*, Lewis suggests a criterion: "Let us try to discover how far it might be plausible to define a good book as a book which is read in one way, and a bad book as a book which is read in another. . . . [The many] are so busy doing things with the work that [they] meet only themselves. . . . If we find that a book is usually read in one way, still more if we never find that it is read in the other, we have a *prima facie* case for thinking it bad." That bad way of reading is to *use*, rather than to *receive*, a book; that is, not to read in the "same spirit as the author writ." Instead, it is to look for biography when the book is poetry, or ideology when it is narrative, or psychology when it is fantasy, and so on. Lewis's point is to respect the experience offered as though it might be very good, giving its own terms the benefit of the doubt.

But just what sort of experience does Lewis himself offer? Aristotle suggests that we best judge a thing according to its own nature. Hence the two most pertinent prior questions: What sort of "book" is C. S. Lewis? and How ought it to be read? Though his personal parliament of geniuses were Will, Imagination, Intellect, and Spirit, the prime minister certainly was Peitho, the goddess of Rhetoric. Adaptation is at the heart of rhetoric, the end of which is always, in the broadest sense, proof. Most at home with a rhetoric of demonstration, Lewis was obliged to elicit belief from particular people, at particular times, under particular circumstances. He epitomized the rhetor as defined by that old Roman teacher Quintilian, in his *Institutes of Oratory*: "the good man speaking well." That is the sort of book we would receive.

To be sure, there are some surprises: Lewis did *not* know himself as thoroughly as he seemed to (there is that rhetorical genius again, concealing as well as revealing). Thus the literary and intellectual contexts are necessarily joined by the biographical. Necessarily, first, because Lewis used himself as an example so profligately in his books, establishing an unmistakably distinctive and appealing voice; and second, as Walter Hooper is right to remind us in his introduction to Lewis's diary, because "life is more richly-textured—or as Lewis would put it, 'thicker'—than we expect it to be. None of us is either this or that; rather we and all the 'ordinary' people we meet and know are many things at once, full of shading and nuance."

Furthermore, Lewis would not so much attempt to argue for the tenets of Christianity as to establish its coherence, and thus its plausibility. Starting from ordinary experience, an extraordinary and nuanced self, and addressing ordinary people, he used the lessons he had learned to equip his readers with their own interpretive instruments, thereby to discover the next world in this one; frankly, to *regress*, as though to a place of origin for which they have always longed. Basic to this enterprise is the premise that each of us must "take the road right out of the self" if we are to become, not "creatures of God but sons of God." Lewis would have us be *fugitives*, as he himself was. Towards this end he would argue, reconcile, sympathize, browbeat, confess, or (ostensibly) withdraw as the particular circumstances warranted.

What would Lewis say, if anything, about "present concerns"? The question is tempting. Our rampant verbicide would surely vex him. The phrase "pro-choice" might stir him, as it does me, to ask, "Don't you really mean pro-*one*-choice, at the expense of every other choice the aborted baby would have made?" But here the contemporary commentator must take care: Though Lewis had reservations about abortion, they were in fact many fewer than some, myself included, might like. "Relationship?" Well, you have a "relationship" with your socks every time you put them on. If you mean "friendship," or "romance," or even the euphemistic "affair," then say so. Or "significant *other*?" In the semantically severe way Lewis had, we seek clarification: for example, do not homosexuals desire a significant *same*? Finally, I can readily see that charges of sexism would be countered with a confession and proclamation or with a countercharge of *virophobia*. Or is this all simply one author's attempt to co-opt the great man's benediction?

In any event, we can note that in fact he unearthed the most influential of our unexamined assumptions: a monomaniacal devotion to "practicality" and a superstitious faith in the inevitability of "progress." He would cite both of these, for example, in discussions of the prospect of cloning human beings for experimental purposes, a misapprehension and misapplication of "equality," and a deep impatience with and suspicion of reason (a version of Wayne Booth's "substition"), as he did in "Modern Man and His Categories of Thought." Of course, bringing us to our senses is one thing—most religious thinkers are moralists, too—but making policy suggestions is quite another. It is likely that he would be mute on the latter and uncharitable towards no one.

He certainly would not be mute on Mere Christianity or its corollaries. He would remind us that we must choose to be either "Man or Rabbit," a being wanting and trying to know or one that simply wants the carrot of efficacy; or that we cannot assent to, let alone give, a sermon and then at lunch belie its lesson with uncharitable behavior; or that when considering "The Trouble with 'x' . . .", we must consider x's personhood, the charity it requires, and our membership in the same Body as x. In short, he would continue to act upon the distinction made by the psychotherapist Phillip Rieff, that "religious man was born to be saved; psychological man was born to be pleased." He would, because he knew that "evangelization," as Pope John Paul II writes in *Crossing the Threshold of Hope*, is the "encounter of the Gospel with the culture of each epoch." And so even when "topical," as in "On Living in an Atomic Age," Lewis is timeless: our "minds claim to be spirit," and "it is part of our spiritual law never to put survival first," so our survival "must be by honourable and merciful means." In short, he got behind platitudes by creating, out of the ordinary, the *conditions* of belief. And to do so he often turned himself into a *datum* by an act of will, distilling from his own hard-fought struggle those qualities most suited to combat, molding them into a posture most likely to be effective, and then deploying them in explicitly personal terms. An arresting blend of argument and appeal, and a figurative richness which animates a verbal world itself organic, together achieve a breadth and depth that add up to more than a mere proposition; they become elements of an intellectual, emotional, and imaginative world bounded by a moral and artistic purpose and incarnating a spiritual vision.

He invites us to participate in that world, to partake of its texture. When we do, we see that what Lewis said of Edmund Spenser is strikingly true of himself and of his world: "His work is one, like a growing thing, a tree ... with branches reaching to heaven and roots to hell. ... And between these two extremes comes all the multiplicity of human life. ... To read him is to grow in mental health." In Lewis's world, the irrational bases of modern disbelief are cleared away. How, in looking at the whole of Lewis, can we not apprehend his greatest accomplishment, that reconstitution of meaning, of connectedness, to which I have referred? When brilliance and intellectual authority; reason, reasonableness, and reliability; tradition, doctrine, and the promise of glory all cohere in the reader—a "machine meant to run on God"—the allure must be irresistible. Would it not be engaging, then, to establish the sources of his appeal? The question is bound to arise (at this centenary and for long thereafter) and, like any rising tide, help lift us all above our and all mere zeitgeists—into the tides of timelessness.

PART I

ROOTS

1

Will

CLIVE STAPLES LEWIS was "a genius of the will," according to the late Owen Barfield, his lifelong friend and solicitor. What exactly Barfield meant is difficult to say; in the context of his seminal introduction to Gibb's *Light on C. S. Lewis* (1965), he is referring to the choice of a persona, a stance chosen for the purposes of public debate. But he goes on to say that, at a certain point in the mid-1930s, Lewis simply stopped caring about his *self* as such, except for its training and straitening: "[H]e deliberately ceased to take any interest in himself except as a kind of spiritual alumnus taking his moral finals." Of course, there is a paradox here. Will is central to the self, perhaps its dominant feature. How, then, may one exercise will in order to subordinate the self, if the exercise of that will necessarily strengthens the self it would otherwise constrict?

For one reason or another, Lewis would spend most of his life contending with this dilemma. The pivotal act of will of Lewis's life is clear, an act that only slightly precedes Barfield's attribution of what we might oxymoronically denominate "willed selflessness." In his preface to *Mere Christianity* (1952) Lewis allowed, "ever since I became a Christian [1931] I have thought that the best, perhaps the only, service I could do for my unbelieving neighbors was to explain and defend the belief that has been common to nearly all Christians at all times." Precisely here is that willed commitment to a vocation, a supremely rhetorical vocation that would require Lewis to deploy the self he must escape. The world-famous apologist, the providential voice, emerged from that choice, for thereafter Lewis never ceased to exercise his vocation, which is what Austin Farrer said being a Christian is all about. A mighty engine indeed must have been the will that drove it.

I

On his father's side eloquence was a prominent feature of professional and of family life. Albert Lewis was born in Cork, but five years later his family moved to Belfast. From 1877 to 1879 he attended the District Model National School, where he was taught by the master W. T. Kirkpatrick, who greatly encouraged his interests in reading and writing. Though he qualified as a solicitor in 1885, he had been in 1881 elected a member of the Belmont Literary Society. Albert's rhetorical ability must have been formidable, for not only did Kirkpatrick retain him ("Woe to the poor juryman who wants to have any mind of his own. He will find himself borne down by a restless Niagara."), but he became the Sessional Solicitor of the Belfast City Council, of the Belfast and County Down Railway Company, and of the National Society for the Prevention of Cruelty to Children. His effectiveness as a political speaker for the Conservative Party was often noted in the press.

So young Jacksie should have surprised no one with his

garrulousness. "See that he does not talk too much," wrote Albert Lewis to his older son, Warren, who had charge of his little brother when the two traveled from their home in Belfast to England.

Lewis read Beatrix Potter's *Squirrel Nutkin* before age five and by the age of eight had written up Animal-Land, which with Warren's "India" became the world of Boxen, a land populated by dressed and talking animals. Letter-writing, too, was an important form of communication within the family, its skilled practice taken seriously; knowing this, Lewis would make a game of his correspondence by sometimes including a letter to his pet mouse, Tommy, when writing to Warren. When not writing, he was enjoying the solitude afforded by the huge Little Lea, the family home to which he was confined by frequent bad weather. He was with the family library as most children are with toys and chocolates, and no book in the house was forbidden to him. In these early years we see the beginning of Lewis's habit of maintaining very long lists of books already read and to-be-read. He took to his mother's earnest tutoring in French and Latin with alacrity.

A decisive balance of rigorous submission and nearly unbounded autonomy was struck in the young man's intellectual life during his late adolescent years. Greek and Latin language and much classical literature came under his ready command, and his judgment was honed by the ruthless dialectical grind provided by W.T. Kirkpatrick, whose student Lewis became, having succeeded his father. On his own he read widely, indiscriminately, and unself-consciously in English literature.

He wrote all about his discoveries to his father and, more openly, to his brother; but real intimacy was shared with Arthur Greeves, a neighbor. Lewis has attributed the learning of a number of lessons to Greeves, whom he called an example of the "first friend," the alter ego. While a youth, Lewis would write, "How funny that I always prove anything I want in argument with you but never convince you." Though the differences between the two men in almost every respect were striking, the friendship, sustained by correspondence, lasted fifty years, ending only with Lewis's death. In these letters, Lewis's enthusiasm and energy, his disinterested voracity and responsiveness, his refusal to distinguish qualitatively between literary experience and experience-at-large are vividly revealed. Each of these qualities is present in a letter to Greeves that describes the momentous event of Lewis's first reading, in 1916, of George MacDonald's *Phantastes*:

> I have had a great literary experience this week. . . . The book is Geo. MacDonald's *Phantastes*, which I picked up by hazard. Have you read it? At any rate whatever you are reading now, you simply must get this at once. . . . Of course it is hopeless for me to try and describe it, but when you have followed the hero Anodos along the little stream of the faery wood, have heard about the terrible ash tree . . . and heard the episode of Cosmo, I know you will agree with me. You must not be disappointed at the first chapter, which is rather conventional faery tale style, and after it you won't be able to stop until you finish. There are one or two poems in the tale, which, with one or two exceptions, are shockingly bad, so don't *try* to appreciate them.

After training with the Great Knock, Lewis would have read, for honors in Classics at Oxford, the classical histories, moral and political philosophy, metaphysics, and faculty psychology; Bacon's works would have been prominent and modern logic emphasized. With the exceptions of Book x in

Quintilian's *Institutes* and of Cicero's *Oratore*, no classical rhetorical or poetic theory was required. Given Lewis's choice to be tested in the history of Roman poetry and in Latin prose style, and to go on to study modern philosophy and philology, he would not necessarily have read the classical orators, whom he did not have in his library. (He did read much Cicero, whom he thought a great bore.) His logic books (e.g., H.W.B. Joseph's *Introduction to Logic*) are very heavily annotated; his Aristotle's *Rhetoric* not at all. This neglect is revealing in light of Lewis's propensity to annotate heavily almost all of his books. If one lacked an index he would provide it; often a single chapter is summarized to the length of several hundred words, and inevitably Lewis's marginalia are argumentative, usually filling the four blank borders surrounding the printed text. He simply, and ironically, did not lend himself to rhetorical theory with the same characteristic thoroughness that marked his other reading.

When not arguing with a text he would contend with classmates, students, colleagues, and friends, craving live, rational opposition. When Lewis first began University College he was one of only twelve students to belong to the Martlets, a venerable literary society at meetings of which a member would read a paper to colleagues and guests. Almost invariably he assumed a "fighting stance," unfashionably defending William Morris, for example, or attacking the theory of poetry as self-expression. It was during such a discussion that Lewis attacked *vers libre* by way of defending, for the first time, his beloved Edmund Spenser's *Faerie Queene*. Minutes were kept—and in Chaucerian Verse! This excerpt is by Nevill Coghill, who would become a great friend of Lewis's; it summarizes Lewis's position on the poem and on poetry and captures his stance as well:

He well could sing, and make his verses grow
One to another, like a forest row
Of deepening trees; no drama, but a mood
Of queer archaic dream, and spacious flow
Of changing rhythms, till then not understood.
He was a pioneer, that did not cut, but plant a wood.
And his sweet satisfying poesy
Offers no problem to the gnawing mind,
But pours the balm of pure simplicity
In allegories as old as is mankind;
Vague and indefinite, they lie behind
The purpose of the poem; for all speech
Of men is allegory, ill-defined
Spenserian and dim: and who can teach
How fact and symbol are related to each?
Young dreamy boys delight in Spenser's lore
And eat his satisfying Faery food
And Wordsworth on his native mountain shore
Caught echoes from that dim enchanted wood;
Then enter ye who dare, ye who have understood.

The combative stance was encouraged by the university tutorial system, which requires a student to write an essay each week and to defend it to his tutor. As an undergraduate and, soon after, as a philosophy tutor himself, Lewis flourished under the system, just as he had flourished under Kirkpatrick's dialectical rigor.

In 1923 Lewis took his third First and won the coveted Chancellor's Prize for an English essay; still, finding a position was very difficult, and he was chosen to deputize in philosophy for E. F. Carritt only after his applications for an English fellowship had been refused. Philosophy was the ideal subject for Lewis at the time. His notebooks reveal, especially with respect to Locke, Hume, Berkeley, and Kant (whom he found very convincing), the same analytical and argumentative temper evidenced by the philosophers themselves; his "provisional critiques" show a forbidding command of method and, as we would expect, a wide learning. Nor did he ever fail to distinguish between analysis and description, on the one hand, and argument (usually refutative) on the other; and he took seriously the word "provisional," for at the time he had no fixed position of his own, other than atheism.

Live opposition was provided by Owen Barfield, whom Lewis called the ideal "second friend," or the anti-self who recognizes as important all the right questions but answers them all wrong: Is imagination a reliable source of truth? Has human consciousness evolved for the worse? Is the frontier between subject and object absolute? By way of a copious correspondence and long, technical, and learned treatises, the "Great War," as they dubbed it, was waged; Lewis would admit, rightly, that Barfield had changed his mind more than he Barfield's. The argument, ostensibly over the occult discipline devised by Rudolph Steiner and known as Anthroposophy, ended when Lewis became a Christian; he then lost all interest in the subject.

Ten years later Lewis would help found the Oxford University Socratic Club, where Christians welcomed and responded to the rational opposition. Lewis was its first president, and because of him the Socratic became the most famous Oxford society of its day. Not only was the opposition live but ferocious as well. When Lewis was on the bill, the atmosphere was sure to be "gladiatorial," and most other university activities would pass virtually unnoticed. During this period (World War II), he toured Royal Air Force bases to speak to airmen on Christianity and became a famous broadcaster with his talks on Christianity over the BBC.

During all of Lewis's life, then, there ran through his personality the rich ores of dazzling eloquence, intellectual mili-
tancy, and a desire to enjoy them both in argument. Any
voluble self can, of course, conceal as well as reveal. Dwelling in a landscape of mountains, hills, valleys, and forests of
speech and of silence, C. S. Lewis reveled, hid, thought, and
eventually would pray. But mostly he argued—a pronouncedly
intellectual means of imposing one's will. And he certainly
enjoyed the presence of an audience. The late John Wain,
novelist, biographer, and former Lewis pupil, has written re-
vealingly of his tutor:

> All these people I admired . . . were all dramatic person-
> alities, making a strong impact. None of them bore any
> resemblance to the ordinary, commonplace, faceless citi-
> zen. Each had a characteristic style, not merely of writ-
> ing or thinking but a style of presenting himself to the
> outside world. They attracted me because in their
> different ways they all treated life as if it were an art. I
> do not mean that they posed. They simply recognized,
> intuitively, that the presence of other people, even the
> humblest and fewest, constitutes an audience, and towards
> an audience one has certain duties. They are always giving
> a performance in the role for which they have cast them-
> selves, making up the play as they go along, and tacitly
> inviting others to collaborate. . . . It is no mere matter of
> posing, of permitting oneself to trifle or be insincere.
> Rather it is the recognition of a duty that is binding on
> everyone, but one that is instinctively accepted by those
> who fall into this type. . . . Such people are in fact fulfilling
> a moral duty. The Creator . . . has equipped them with
> a certain identity, and they are all the time delightfully
> aware of this identity and out to get, and to give, as much
> fun as possible with it.

Within the boundaries of his "role" Lewis could suit his audience, usually calibrating his weaponry well enough so as not to overkill. Though never patronizing, he could be temperate. But whatever the tone, the mode was almost always argument. "It was not that he expected perfection," wrote Jocelyn Gibb, his editor,

> for he was essentially a kind, tolerant man, but he derived such pleasure in seeing the striving for perfection that one often felt on one's mettle. Lewis, however, was not an exacting person. To engage in conversation with him was stimulating and at the same time comforting. He always brought out the best in people so that you felt you were making as much a contribution as he was to the parry of words. . . . And woe betide you if you made a woolly remark or betrayed an obvious weakness in your argument. He would be on you in a flash; not unkind or rough, but questioning, making you explain your reasons—if you had any.

On the other hand, John Lawlor, one of Lewis's pupils and a friend, is insistent in his dissent from Gibb's description, going so far as to have told me that Lewis often came off as "arrogant," adding that he would welcome being proved wrong. Roger Lancelyn Green echoes these observations. He had been Lewis's pupil, then during the 1950s became a close enough friend to travel with Mrs. Green and Jack and Joy Lewis to Greece on the Lewis's honeymoon trip in 1960, and finally served as Lewis's co-biographer. In response to my question about Lewis's argumentativeness Green wrote, "My recollection is that I never thought about it—which surely means it was not obtrusive." It may have been so with others, Green allows, "but grew less and less so. I only got to know him well during the last 15 years of his life." Green then adds, tellingly

I think, "at first I certainly found an evening with him rather an ordeal—a pleasant ordeal but an exhausting one."

In short, Lewis's "default position" was argument (the record shows no quarrels whatsoever, a quite distinct mode), and he had to adjust—usually down—from there. Though it must be noted that Lawlor is in the minority, such a minority, consisting mostly of former pupils, existed. And as any teacher knows, judgments made by students, who compulsively judge their teachers, are to some degree and in many instances true. And given Wain's judgment, a Lewis uncertain in the presence of an unfamiliar audience should come as no surprise. R. W. Ladborough, Lewis's closest colleague at Cambridge, to which Lewis moved in 1954 upon being offered the professorial chair in Medieval and Renaissance English literature, has described the newcomer's self-consciousness upon entering a strange, and traditionally hostile, environment. He was anxious to be accepted and strived for brilliance because he thought it was expected. With his tweed coat at High Table, booming voice, jolly-farmer appearance, and common tastes, Lewis did come off as something of a poseur.

Barfield has written that "his skill in dialectical obstetrics was greatly furthered by a characteristic . . . which he seems to have shared with Jeremy Bentham . . . a certain delight in expounding the obvious and in expounding it meticulously and more than once." He is probably referring to Lewis's participation in the Inklings, that small group of friends, including J. R. R. Tolkien and Charles Williams, who met regularly in order to talk and to read works in progress to each other. From the start of the tradition immediately before World War II to its end upon Lewis's death, the center of attention was Lewis himself. Warren Lewis has described what might happen when no one had anything to read: "On these occasions the fun would be riotous, with Jack at the top of his form and enjoying every minute . . . an outpouring of wit, nonsense, whimsey, dialectical swordplay, and pungent judgment such as I have rarely seen equaled."

At least one of the sources of such abandon is easy to identify. "Lewis and I spent many hours together," wrote Leo Baker, his first real Oxford friend. Apart from poetry, they "shared two lighter literary interests." Of lesser importance were the novels of H. Rider Haggard.

> The other, most important, indeed almost an obsession, was the book by that leprechaun James Stephens, *The Crock of Gold*. Here we found a food we both needed: an amalgam of humour, poetry, myth, philosophy, and, above all, imagination. I have no doubt that Lewis was quite deeply influenced by this book. We knew chunks of it by heart and quoted from it delightedly when words or events presented an opportunity. Even now the thought of the Thin Woman of Inis Magrath, or even more the so-often repeated negative, 'I will not, said the Philosopher,' conjures up Lewis's young face grinning.

This exuberant yet melancholy, beckoning yet untamed, comically metaphysical oxymoron-of-a-book would seem to have been written particularly for the enjoyment of C. S. Lewis. He and Baker, he and Owen Barfield, and he and Charles Williams, and J. R. R. Tolkien—Lewis and any one, or two, or five—could have been the two Philosophers. Stephens describes them:

> To them there were only two kinds of sounds anywhere— these were conversation and noise: they liked the first very much indeed, but they spoke of the second with stern disapproval. "Do you know . . . that a leprechaun came here

today? Are you going to listen to what I am telling you about the leprechaun?" said the Thin Woman. "I am not," said the philosopher.... "Will you ever be done talking?" shouted the Thin Woman passionately. "I will not," said the Philosopher. "In certain ways sleep is useful. It is an excellent way of listening to an opera or seeing pictures on a bioscope. If you were going to say anything, love, please say it now, but you should always remember to think before you speak.... Children should always be in bed. These are serious truths, which cannot be controverted....

His rollicking affection is symptomatic: these various "truths" about women and children are, of course, exaggerations of Lewis's own temperamental predispositions; but to some degree they were at least his settled preferences through most of his young middle age. The opinion about conversation, however, is no exaggeration, was more than a mere preference, and remained so until Lewis died.

II

With its story-telling intensity, love of good talk, evocative natural beauty, and close-knit good faith, Ireland was and remains a difficult land not to be happy in and influenced by. Lewis was both. His Irishness has been little remarked upon, except by Lewis himself, who, with no trace of cultural fetishism, never forgot his Irish roots. On the one hand, he would remind an inquirer who asked his opinion of Cromwell that, after all, he, Lewis, was an Irishman; on the other, Irish mythology was only his third favorite, after Norse and Classical. But he always returned to Ireland to walk, to visit, and to reread James Stephens, who was an Irish patriot and poet, as well as the author of *The Crock of Gold*. And if he lacked his brother's unbounded enthusiasm for their home country, he nevertheless understood that he had inhaled its air irremediably. He once reminded a friend that among his reasons for not having become a Roman Catholic were his inbred Ulster Protestant prejudices, with respect to which he considered himself utterly typical.

When he was a little boy still living in the first family house, Lewis lost his dog Jacksie in an accident. He immediately designated himself Jacksie and would then answer to no other name. To his friends he would be Jack Lewis the rest of his life. (Perhaps he really did turn down the knighthood offered by Churchill's government in order to avoid being called Sir Clive.) The middle-aged Lewis would claim that he was raised in a nominally Christian household, but merely "nominal" seems not to have been the case at all. His mother's family, the Hamiltons, included many an illustrious clergyman and theologian, an archbishop, and at least one preacher of some repute, Lewis's grandfather, Thomas Hamilton. Religious practice in the household was maintained with ease and without hypocrisy. To a child, of course, this would not have been particularly salient or noteworthy. What is the case is that he was preternaturally happy. The mature Lewis would say "My childhood, at all events, was not in the least other-worldly. It lives in my memory mainly as a period of humdrum, prosaic happiness." Not only was he secure in his class and surrounded by loving family—included in the Irishness, and thus in the happiness and influence, were of course Flora (Florence Augusta Hamilton) and Albert (James) Lewis, Jacksie's parents— but he had things largely his own way.

His brother Warnie (Warren Hamilton Lewis), older than Jacksie by three years, allowed the younger boy to take the lead in play, since Jacksie had the more ample imagination by far and most of their games involved invention of one sort or another. He could write the stories he wished to write, contriving imaginary countries of his own choosing, and when, in 1905, the family moved to Little Lea in Strandtown, right outside of Belfast, he had the unrestricted run—as he did of his father's formidable library—of the huge, complicated edifice, with its long corridors, hidden passageways, and little back room. This independence was important to the boy, for as much as anything else he often wished for solitude, again on his own terms. In short, if he was left alone, it was because that is exactly what he desired.

A second desire early joined the first. A small toy garden built into a can, the autumn of Beatrix Potter's *Squirrel Nutkin*, and above all the distant Castlereagh, or "Green," Hills would each in turn arouse a strong, painful longing in the boy. He believed it a message from elsewhere, beckoning him to a place just beyond his reach, a place elusive and finally lost. He would misspend, by various acts of his formidable will, much time, effort, and virtue in chasing back this desire, which he dubbed Joy, or *Sehnsucht*. His search for it, along with the shafts of Joy themselves, came to an end upon the recovery of his Christian faith. Only then did he cease trying to will the event, in essence an internal emotional state of the imperial self—that same self which, remember, he was seeking on other grounds to put in its place, by that "willed selflessness"—since he now knew whence it came and how to get there. But for that little boy the need for any conversion, let alone the conversion itself, lay in the future; security, solitude, and Joy were sufficiently at hand for him to be happy, and to take settled happiness for granted.

By any account the ground of that settled happiness, Flora

Lewis, was a remarkable woman. She attended The Royal University of Ireland (now Queen's University, Belfast), where she passed with First Class Honours in Geometry and Algebra in 1881 and, in 1885, with First Class Honours in Logic and Second Class Honours in Mathematics. She received her B.A. in 1886.

When she was twelve, the future logician, during a visit to a Catholic church in Rome, where her father was chaplain of Holy Trinity church, became fascinated by the body of a young female saint enclosed in a glass case. Upon gazing at the body a second time, Flora would write, the saint "slowly lifted her eyelids and looked at me; I was terribly frightened and felt myself getting cold—I had hardly time to look at or admire her large blue eyes when she closed them again." This narrative ability resurfaced in 1889 when she published a story called "The Princess Rosetta" in the *Household Journal* of London. Albert raved about it. She, having turned down Albert's first marriage proposal in 1886, accepted his second in June of 1893.

Flora Lewis died on August 23, 1908, six days before the Lewis's fourteenth wedding anniversary. She was forty-six years old; Jacksie not quite ten. Of course, Lewis discussed this episode in *Surprised by Joy*: His mother's death was like a continent sinking beneath the sea, bringing with it the end of all settled happiness. But with very few and very brief exceptions he seems never otherwise to have mentioned it. The implications of the end of his settled happiness—and the possibility that others, too, may have had their happiness thoroughly unsettled—simply did not occupy him. For example, he showed no understanding of, let alone sympathy for, a father who was not only bereft of his great love—for the romance shared by Flora and Albert seems to have been deep, rich, and palpable—but left virtually alone with the daunting task of raising two young sons.

More significant, however, is the older autobiographer's inattention to the implications of young Jacksie's experience of his mother's death. Knowing that she lay dying in the next room, the boy prayed to a father in heaven, a magician-god, as he would call him, who failed to answer his prayers; the unsettling was complete when, very shortly after Flora's death, young Jack only then for the first time left home and went off to school. Amidst the prolonged and intense misery which was his stay at Wynyard School—little more than a prison presided over by a sadist who, before dying, would be clinically certified as insane—Lewis began to love England, learned gregariousness (especially in the form of a small band standing loyally against a common enemy), and first became an effective believer, seriously praying, reading the Bible, and attending to doctrine earnestly but unhysterically taught. This was during the years 1909 and 1910, when he was on the verge of puberty. In seriously attempting to obey his conscience, he discovered nothing that he would have denied already believing as a result of his "nominally Christian" upbringing. But soon the boy clamped down upon his emotions—they would be avenged—with all his strength of will; and the man utterly refused to attribute his putative atheism to the failure of this sky-magician to save his mother or to the willingness of a loving God to snatch her away. For the very first time, Lewis's will had been seriously controverted, and its response was decisive: Though not immediate, rejection was complete.

The study of the effects on children of early parental loss—much like the use of a vocabulary that includes "denial"—smacks of "over-elaborated psychologism à la mode our twentieth-century rococo," as Owen Barfield put it. But surely this is distinguishable from psychology *per se*, a systematic study of collective experience in the literature of the field. There we are told that *delay* often marks pre-adolescents who have lost a parent. Mourning itself may be delayed, leading to school phobias, the search for a relationship analogous to the one lost, and distortions and strictures of the young personality.

The child's development may be fixed at the stage it occupied at the loss, in which case the emerging identity—the answer to the question, Who am I?—is also much delayed, very often until the entire traumatic event is recapitulated. Working harder to avoid suffering than to achieve delight, the child also delays long-term romantic love far beyond the normal span of time. Nightmares are common; shame and guilt, often in the company of embarrassment at expressions of pity, result in an intolerance of pain and sadness. Conversions often occur, and we must remember that a denial of religious faith is no less a conversion than its recovery. And there is anger at the surviving parent, especially in cases where that parent is ineffectual in coping with the loss. Lewis's early life, and to a lesser degree his middle life, evidence the classic symptoms of early parental loss almost paradigmatically.

Lewis loathed his schools. He may have exaggerated their torments, as Warren, who had been to the same schools, claimed. But torments there were, and Lewis did not endure them well. On the other hand, he flourished under the tutelage of W. T. Kirkpatrick, who taught him—and Albert and Warren before him—Greek, Latin, and a dialectical method so severe that any tendency to platitude and habit of facile, unexamined assumption were thoroughly rinsed out. When Kirkpatrick died in 1921, Jack wrote to Albert of the master's "unrelenting clearness and rigid honesty of thought. If ever a man came near to being a purely logical entity, that man was

Kirk. The idea that human beings should exercise their vo-
cal organs for any purpose except that of communicating or
discovering truth was to him preposterous. The most casual
remark was taken as a summons to disputation." Kirkpatrick,
an atheist, could not but have reinforced Lewis's own atheism,
though he would not have countenanced what Lewis would
later call his "blaspheming" atheism. By the end of his time
with Kirkpatrick, Lewis was among the best-prepared candi-
dates for admission to Oxford University, but because he, the
son of a mathematical mother, failed Responsions, substan-
tially an algebra test, he was denied that admission.

Why Lewis enlisted in the army in World War I really is
anybody's guess; his motives must have been as mixed as
motives usually are. The waiving of the Responsions require-
ment may have been among them. He might have wanted to
hurt Albert, or to please him, for by now they were estranged.
Or perhaps he thought it his duty: We do know that as an
Irishman he was exempt from the draft. Billeted at Oxford
University for training, Lewis and Paddy (Edward Francis
Courtenay) Moore met before they shipped out to the front.
At this time Lewis met and enjoyed the hospitality of Paddy's
mother, Janie King Moore, or "Minto," as Lewis would later
dub her, and of Paddy's younger sister Maureen. There was a
Mr. Moore, Courtenay Edward, but he remained in Ireland.
The marriage was an unhappy one, but the two were never
divorced. The young men, each with a single parent and both
facing the concrete possibility of death, cut a deal: If one were
killed, the other would assure the well-being of the dead
comrade's family. As both Albert and Warren would later note,
this was an absurdity on Lewis's part: He was in no position
to assure anything, on the one hand, and, on the other, Albert,
quite unlike Mrs. Moore, would hardly need someone else's
financial support if his son were to be killed in action.

The horrors of the Great War were new horrors for which no participant could have been prepared. John Keegan, in *The Face of Battle*, vividly depicts the nature of trench warfare. The sheer weight of fire from field guns and, especially, machine guns was enough to keep infantrymen in their trenches, knee-deep in mud and often in the muck of their stricken comrades. Because of the complexity of the trenches, men were often blown up by their own grenades. In one attack at the dreaded Somme, the British lost twenty-one thousand men, most in the first minutes of the attack. Keegan quotes Robert Kee, who called the trenches "the concentration camps of the First World War." Keegan, describing the prototypical Battle of the Somme, observes that "there is something Treblinka-like about . . . those long docile lines of young men, shoddily uniformed, heavily burdened, numbered about their necks, plodding forward across a featureless landscape to their own extermination inside the barbed wire." Keegan's eyewitness accounts of combat in the Great War are often literally unbearable.

For his own part, Lewis captured several dozen German prisoners, being humorously scolded by his sergeant for not having drawn his pistol in the process (apparently the Germans were only too happy to be captured by the English rather than the French), saw that same sergeant blown to bits in close proximity, and was himself seriously wounded. "This is war," he would write. "This is what Homer wrote about." In any event, it was Paddy who did not return.

We now see full-blown the putative bifurcation of Lewis's psyche that he would make a major motif in his autobiography. He would designate these two parts the Inner and Outer lives, the former marked by his search for Joy, the latter by intellectual development and by quotidian life in general. Many see this as a great divide between his imagination and his reason, but I do not believe that particular divide to have

been greater in Lewis than in most of us. Rather, it was a divide
between the profoundly troubled spirit seeking to address its
considerable pain and the strong-willed genius who would
deny it. Furthermore, there was not just one divide. The Lewis
returning from the Great War was a young man sorely out of
sync, ignoring his university obligation to live in college, false
to the code of conduct in which he had been raised, and ly-
ing to his alienated father.

But he was true to his compact with Paddy: Lewis set up
house with Mrs. Moore and Maureen. Working to hold a
house—that is, to "husband" it—he was too young and im-
mature to know what was required, let alone to do it. But for
the generous and thoroughly deceived Albert he would have
been utterly impoverished. Once he was finally compelled to
buy trousers because the one pair he already owned bordered
upon immodesty; on another occasion he could afford only
a single razor blade. This near-penury issued from Mrs.
Moore's virtual indigence. As the menage progressed, the liaison of Lewis and this handsome woman in her late forties
almost certainly included a brief sexual interlude, but the
anomalous household ended only with the death of Mrs. Moore
on January 12, 1951, at the age of seventy-nine. Lewis's willingness, until nearly the very end, abruptly to undertake a flow
of menial chores warranted Mrs. Moore's observation that he
was as good "as having an extra servant." Christopher Derrick, a pupil of Lewis's, has remarked on this episode and on
Lewis's later marriage to Joy Davidman that they represented
in his friend a strain of *Weiberherrschaft*, a sort of self-inden-
turing to certain women. More generally, Lewis's father,
brother, and his great friend J. R. R. Tolkien took Derrick's
notion one step further, but in a somewhat different direction,
by arguing that Lewis was unable to resist *anyone* in need.

In such matters he was self-indulgent *and* unself-conscious, and would have others be the same. As he says of his friend Arthur Greeves,

> During the early years of our acquaintance he was (as always) a Christian, and I was an atheist. But though (God forgive me) I bombarded him with all the thin artillery of a seventeen year old rationalist, I never made any impression on his faith. He remains victor in that debate. It is I who have come round. The thing is sym- bolical of much in our joint history. He was not a clever boy; he was even a dull boy; I was a scholar. He had no "ideas". I bubbled over with them. It might seem that I had much to give him, and that he had nothing to give me. But this is not the truth. I could give concepts, logic, facts, arguments, but he had feelings to offer, feelings which more mysteriously—for he was always very inarticulate—he taught me to share. Hence, in our com- merce, I dealt in superficies, but he in solids. . . . I learned charity from him and failed, for all my efforts, to teach him arrogance in return.

Virgil became one of his favorite authors (and his very favorite classical author), but most pagans over-indulge cer- tain appetites. To this general rule Lewis proved no excep- tion, the appetite proving to be sexual. The first woman after whom he "lusted" was the dancing mistress at Cherbourg House, his second school, where he abandoned Christianity and became swaggering and priggish. There appear to have been other attachments accompanied by an active adolescent fantasy life along the way; and Lewis seems not to have exer- cised very much self-control. After befriending Arthur in September 1914, the two boys shared their fantasies which, by the time Lewis turned eighteen, took an odd turn. In a letter of January 31, 1917, he wonders if the beloved William Morris might not be "a special devotee of the rod" and whether the soul of one of Arthur's female relatives might not be improved if the body were punished. That is one of the letters he signed "Philomastix." "I am given to understand," he tells Arthur, "that the idea of suffering yourself appeals to you more than that of inflicting. It used to be so with me, and perhaps the experienced victim does get a more vivid, voluptuous sensation than the operator—at first. But of course once you are really in pain you can't think of anything else while the operator grows keener all the time." These references, regular at first, then increasingly less frequent, make clear that the punishment ought to be mild, applied to the woman's buttocks, "one of the most beautiful parts" of the body.

Within a year expressions of this preference cease, though past-tense allusions to them, and to other sexual matters, would continue, infrequently, until Lewis's conversion. In the meanwhile Lewis became a vehemently sarcastic, "blaspheming" atheist: one who received the sacraments of Confirmation and Communion without the slightest shred of belief and then thought it "extremely telling to call God *Jahveh* and Jesus *Yeshua*." In his university days he read much Freud and Havelock Ellis; later he would dream of seductive "brown girls" (a purely symbolic, not racial, coloration) and allow that he had greatly underestimated the ease of overcoming the sin of lust.

From his diary, *All My Road Before Me: The Diary of C.S. Lewis, 1922-1927*, we learn that the man who is not yet the "converted pagan living among apostate Puritans" was repulsed by a reminder of Maureen's first Holy Communion, "this most Uncomfortable [*sic*] sacrament," that her Confirmation was like "the slaughtering of a pig," and that he had "never sunk so low" in combat as to pray. He was beset both by recurring headaches and unsettling dreams—about his mother, an arranged marriage, and his blaspheming response; about attempted stabbings, during which he "behaved like the prig hero of an adventure story"; and about "aesthetes of Satanic sneer," one of whom he converted! All the while he nourished friendships, worked hard toward his degree and the fellowship he saw at rainbow's end, and did several good deeds. Not the least of these was helping a neighboring young woman escape the physical abuse of her parents; nearly the most daunting was his helping to keep watch over and control the Doc, Mrs. Moore's brother, who spent two harrowing weeks going mad.

Lewis says nothing of Mrs. Moore in his mid-life autobiography, refusing to discuss one long, "complex episode." Not even from Warnie would he brook any mention of it, let alone discuss it. Many good friends took Mrs. Moore to be his mother, which is how he introduced her and commonly referred to her. But what he does say of himself in the autobiography seems borne out by the earlier diary—until a second look reveals otherwise. A third life, the Official, exists alongside the Inner and Outer that he posits. It was "self-regarding," as the Outer is described in the autobiography, but Joy hardly makes an appearance. His astonishing intellectual life is at least adumbrated, but not the clarifying and influential "Great War" that he conducted with Owen Barfield over the axioms and conclusions of Anthroposophy. (This omission from the diary was noted with considerable surprise by Barfield.) Lewis's Outer life during this period simply was not the Outer life recalled in the later autobiography: it does not seem, either to the reader *or to the diarist*, especially "grim and meaningless," as he would characterize it some thirty years later.

We realize that we are reading an official story when we learn
that Mrs. Moore was the primary audience for the diary entries: Lewis would read them aloud to her. Of course, she—
unlike readers of the autobiography—learns nothing of the
crucial Inner life. Now, it is utterly impossible that Lewis himself was unaware of it, or merely inattentive to it. Did he then
repress it? Hardly: The Inner life simply did not fit the Official
Story nor suit its overseer, just as the menage itself required
a cover story—residential undergraduate life—to deceive
Albert. True, so to speak, to this dishonesty is the diarist's
failure even to mention the book that was among the most
influential on the Inner life. G. K. Chesterton is praised in
Surprised by Joy as having "more sense than all the other
moderns put together; bating, of course, his Christianity."
There Lewis ascribes a pivotal role to Chesterton's *The Everlasting Man*, which showed that "Christianity itself was very
sensible 'apart from Christianity.'" But there is no mention
of the book in the diary, and we can note that among the several references to Chesterton the most suggestive is the one
he fails to make.

A chart of this psychological redoubt is fascinating. It
includes the interplay of the death of Lewis's mother; his resentment of his father, who, along with God the Father, failed
to save his mother; Mrs. Moore, a mother-surrogate, an instrument of punishment, even of revenge, upon his father, and
a willing partner in the *Weiberherrschaft* he alludes to in his
correspondence with Arthur Greeves; and his narrative poem
Dymer, wherein "a man . . . on some mysterious bride, begets
a monster: which monster, as soon as it has killed its father,
becomes a God," as Lewis himself summarized its plot. Each

of the nine cantos consists of from thirty-two to thirty-six stanzas, with each stanza containing seven lines. The entire poem is 1,883 lines long. It does not arrest the reader's attention, though with respect to the verse there are long stretches of real virtuosity. In his preface to the 1950 edition, Lewis wrote of the impact which Mussolini was having on the European imagination and of the influence of the New Psychology, in which all undergraduates seemed to be drenching themselves. Not only did he admit that psychoanalysts would have a field day with the poem, but in 1926 when it was complete he would write with no apparent sense of irony, "of course *I'm* not Dymer."

I leave it to the reader to count the number of divides, remembering that Lewis admitted to one. But we must agree that only the strongest of wills could hold together the "distortions and strictures" of this personality: an Inner life apart from an Outer one, two related but separate Official stories apart from the first two lives, and a Deeper life, lived by an Unknown Self, that includes the Dormant Christian.

Not-too-roughly speaking, Lewis's liaison with Mrs. Moore began as he was preparing his cycle of lyrics, *Spirits in Bondage*, for publication in 1919, and ended, as such, with his conversion, shortly after the publication of *Dymer*, under the pseudonym Clive Hamilton, in 1926. Part I of the lyrical cycle is entitled "The Prison House" and includes "Dungeon Gates":

> *So piteously the lonely soul of man*
> *Shudders before this universal plan,*
> *So grievous is the burden of the pain,*
> *So heavy weighs the long, material chain*
> *From cause to cause, too merciless for hate,*
>
> . . . .

> *O! but we shall keep*
> *Our vision still, One moment was enough,*
> *We know we are not made of mortal stuff.*
> *And we can bear all trials that come after,*
> *The hate of men and the fool's loud bestial laughter*
> *And Nature's rule and cruelties unclean,*
> *For we have seen the Glory—we have seen.*

Symptomatically, the atheist sought both comfort and license in Mrs. Moore. But the would-be fugitive, still a witness to Joy, remains the poet—an imaginative man—and "imagination is," as Lewis would later have it, "the organ of truth." So he devotes himself to the writing of *Dymer*; and its very last stanza epitomizes the purgative, therapeutic, and catalytic effect that writing the poem must have had on him:

> *And from the distant corner of day's birth*
> *He heard clear trumpets blowing and bells ring,*
> *A noise of great good coming into earth*
> *And such a music as the dumb would sing*
> *If Balder had led back the blameless spring*
> *With victory, with the voice of charging spears,*
> *And in white lands long-lost Saturnian years.*

If Pascal is right that anyone searching for God has already found him, then perhaps anyone who believes himself an atheist is one. But I think not, and though Lewis surely believed it, I do not. His testimonial to Chesterton and to other Christian writers whom he would read—Bunyan, Hooker, and Dante, for example—is, I think, evidence of this. So is his response to MacDonald's *Phantastes*, which he read when he was sixteen and which "baptized his imagination," he said, by teaching him holiness. This is not the talk of an atheist, just as *Dymer* is not the poem of one. It is the talk, as the poem is the work, of a young man with a sorely fractured self. And why not? Nature had wreaked "cruelties unclean" in the cancer it used to kill his mother. Yet he intuits "great good coming into earth" and will assert he is not of "mortal stuff," since he has "seen the Glory" and cannot forget it. He will find the predictable analogous relationship in Mrs. Moore, who will serve two purposes besides, and he will hate and deceive the surviving, ineffectual parent (already having had school phobias and nightmares); but he will nevertheless "bear all trials that come after" and will "keep his vision still," even if he must disguise it from himself—in spite of very great pain and its denial.

Warren Lewis was not only Jack's dearly-beloved brother but his greatest friend as well. First an Army officer trained at Sandhurst, then the editor of the Lewis Family Papers, and finally a historian of the age of Louis xiv, his prose style every bit as engaging as his brother's, Warnie became increasingly dependent upon drink. He had retired with the rank Captain in the early 1930s and, at first reluctantly, came to live with his brother and Mrs. Moore. He was an Inkling, a boatman, a motorcyclist, and a great walker. Perhaps owing to the burden of having to share a household with Mrs. Moore, whom he loathed as much as he would come to love his sister-in-law, Joy Davidman, his alcoholism finally became full-blown and wearisomely debilitating.

His diary has been adroitly edited by Clyde Kilby and Marjorie Mead and published as *Brothers & Friends*. In it we meet a man who is vigilant, reflective, prayerful, and always appreciative. His opinions can be surprising and provocative, as when he saw a production of *Hamlet* and wrote, "There is one admirable character in this, Polonius. . . . but alas all too soon he was killed. . . . As for Hamlet I have rarely conceived such a sudden antipathy to any character. . . . this snivelling, attitudinizing, platitudinizing arch bore. . . ." After all, Polonius

was a family man, doing his best by his daughter, and Warren loved home and family above all else. He never failed to
return to his own genuine core: Little Lea, and Jacksie,
"Mammy," and "Pappy."

Indeed, except in the physical sense, the four were never
apart. His recollections of Flora are few but very touching,
especially those that precede his brother's birth but include
Albert. As these memories combine with others Albert's true
character emerges. For example, he was not actually cruel to
his own father, as the boys believed, but tempered in his response to a man who was himself horribly cruel. Was he
thoughtless in not having a stained glass window erected in
memory of his wife? Warren learns otherwise, and accumu-
lated scales of disapprobation instantly fall away. For if Albert
was something of a Polonius himself, he was also the man who
was solemnly praised by Kirkpatrick on the occasion of Flora's
death for being true to himself, "no slight achievement," he
wrote, "in the estimate of all who know the facts."

At first Janie King Moore and her daughter Maureen and
Lewis did not co-habitate, but he very much filled the position of a son and soon simply took them over as his family.
To Albert Lewis she was Mrs. Moore, and he did not "know
what to do about Jack's affair. It worries and depresses me
greatly"; he proceeds: "All I know about the lady is that she is
old enough to be his mother, and that she is in poor circumstances. I also know that Jacks has frequently drawn cheques
in her favour running up to £10—for what I don't know. If
Jacks were not an impetuous kind-hearted creature who could
be cajoled by any woman who had been through the mill, I
should not be so uneasy."

Some short time after Flora's death, the emotional distance
began to grow between Lewis and his father, a highly rhetorical,

intrusive homebody. Not at all a tyrant, Albert was sentimental and in need of much support. Unpublished letters from Flora to Albert make clear that during family vacations in which Albert would not share he needed to be "consoled" by letters which he almost never answered. He would virtually whine if he did not receive them in a timely fashion. Furthermore, his own lush eloquence, which in fact served him so well at the bar and as a local political worker, was a positive nuisance at home, to the extent that it interfered with all meaningful communication between himself and his children. This situation was necessarily aggravated by the fact that Albert took for granted his sons' eagerness to hear him and would therefore intrude himself upon them just as though he were, not a welcome guest, but rather their intellectual salvation. But these errors of commission by Albert took back seat to two errors of omission: Probably through ignorance, he failed to remove Jack from the tortures of his first school in a timely fashion, and through a misunderstanding he failed to see Jack off before he was sent to the front. The later argument over Mrs. Moore, sparked by Albert's having opened a letter addressed to his son, was, given the circumstances, inevitable. The intimacy between Lewis and his father, on the one hand, and between Lewis and Mrs. Moore, on the other, varied inversely.

Nevertheless, casting a reasonable doubt upon the image of Albert Lewis as unmitigated oppressor is not terribly difficult. Lewis himself tries to restore some balance in his account by referring to his father's "fertility, the generosity and humour" of mind. "With the cruelty of youth I allowed myself to be irritated by traits in my father which, in other elderly men, I have since regarded as lovable foibles." Moreover, we have incidents reported by Lewis yet unappreciated by him, as when we hear of how he and Albert quite unself-consciously and earnestly agree that Knock's "one great bad habit—inexcus-able—was that of bending back book-covers to crack the spine." And finally, we know of certain elements about which Lewis knew, or could have known, but did not write. Albert was not merely sentimental but genuinely affectionate; Lewis was "Jacko," who would receive a rare, coveted gift which (un-beknownst to the child) the father had learned he wanted and labored to obtain, and who would receive continued financial support even after he had abandoned his father for a liaison which gave Albert great pain.

To Albert, Warren was always "Badge," in whose place Albert would pay an embarrassingly indiscreet creditor and yet never reveal, nor even allude to, the incident. But this must have been a duty happily discharged. In June 1908, he wrote to Warren of two important matters. The first was that never in his life would he be "disappointed or annoyed with you if you really do your very best. The second is to tell you how pleased I am when you come to me with your troubles. My dear Son, it may be that God in His mercy has decided that you will have no person in the future to come to but me." He was no less than a man who, at age forty-five, lost his wife on his own birthday, his father a few months later, and who then proceeded to do his level best to raise his sons, which must make him not all that bad, even if not downright heroic.

Shortly after the publication of *Dymer*, Lewis virtually reconciled with his father, who had indeed begotten something of a monster—as geniuses of the will are wont to be—on his bride, who surely was exceptional enough as to seem myste-rious. Not long thereafter, on September 24, 1929, Albert died. And the same year the monster became a god; that is, Lewis became a professing, kneeling, praying Theist. By his thirty-third year was instead a Christian. The emotions had, though not completely, avenged themselves, and that is when he ceased paying attention to his self as something to be sated and committed his will—that great engine of choice—to the vocation that would make him the foremost Christian apologist in the English-speaking world and beyond.

Once he stopped arguing with a God in whom he professed disbelief, Lewis had much to pray about and the will to do it ceaselessly. The pain of early parental loss, of trench warfare, and of nearly two decades in the wilderness of spiritual confusion was joined by the pain of the death of Charles Williams, professional disappointment when Oxford failed to give him the professorial Chair he so rightly deserved, growing estrangement from some of his closest friends, particularly Tolkien, when his liaison with Joy Davidman deepened into a rooted, romantic love and then marriage, and the tragic death of Joy herself in 1960 from a recurrence of cancer. That Lewis bore it all so well that many of his friends and acquaintances knew nothing of these episodes is sometimes taken as evidence of Lewis's opaqueness to, if not ignorance of, pain. This is the position, for example, of the fatuous *Shadowlands*, and surely it is nonsense. Rather, this forbearance is further testimony to his genius of will. As early as 1940, in *The Problem of Pain*, Lewis had written, "You would like to know how I behave when I am experiencing pain, not writing books about it. You need not guess, for I will tell you; I am a great coward. . . . When I think of pain . . . it 'quite o'ercrows my spirit'. . . . I am not arguing that pain is not painful. Pain hurts. That is what pain means. . . . [W]hen pain is to be borne, a little courage helps more than much knowledge, a little human sympathy more than much courage, and the least tincture of the love of God more than all."

The genius of the will uses all there is to use to adjust its self to the world, inside and out. In Lewis's case there was pain, rhetorical fluency, and an intellectually militant predisposition. When, in such a man as Lewis, these in part led to, and certainly came to keep company with, spiritual faith and religious belief, the result was that willed commitment to a vocation that he declared in his preface to *Mere Christianity*. The contradiction inherent in that choice—the coupling of "willed selflessness" with the assertive self that is required by the vocation and which Lewis would relish—went unnoticed by Lewis for quite some time and would also take its toll.

There is in psychology a model known as the Johari Window. It depicts the self as a window with four panes: the Open self is *known* to that self *and* to others; the Hidden is known to the self but *not* to others; the Blind is *unknown* to the self but known to others; and the Unknown self, which lives that Deeper life, is *unknown by all*. A provocative model, even if a bit facile. But it is useful to recall that "window" originally meant a glassless "eye to the wind" or, to press the etymological point, to a moving breath, a spirit. Nevertheless, Lewis surely would have preferred Keats's metaphor: "A man's life of any worth is a continual allegory," he wrote, "and very few eyes can see the mystery of his life—a life like the Scriptures, figurative—which . . . people can no more make out than they can the Hebrew Bible."

Lewis himself revealed much, distorted some, and concealed some more. So whether we prefer a psychological model or a poetic metaphor, we must not forget that Lewis was no exception to the principles of either. The consideration of C.S. Lewis's self is a very great challenge. He at once hid it absolutely, distorted it, and invented parts of it to parade forth; he repressed, explored, and denied it; he indulged and overcame it; certainly he would transform, and then transcend it; almost always he used it. And always he coyly warned us against discussing it.

2

Grammar

N EAR THE CLOSE of his own life, Lewis closes his mis-
leadingly modest *An Experiment in Criticism* with
words that are among the most beautiful in all his
work, virtually devotional, utterly illustrative of the wholeness
of his aesthetic, psychological, and spiritual premises—and
deeply revealing of his battle against the imperial self:

> My own eyes are not enough for me, I will see through
> those of others. Reality, even seen through the eyes of
> many, is not enough. I will see what others have invented.
> Even the eyes of all humanity are not enough. I regret
> that the brutes cannot write books. Very gladly would I
> learn what face things present to a mouse or a bee; more
> gladly still would I perceive the olfactory world charged
> with all the information and emotion it carries for a dog.
> Literary experience heals the wound, without undermin-
> ing the privilege, of individuality. There are mass emo-
> tions which heal the wound; but they destroy the
> privilege. In them our separate selves are pooled and we
> sink back into sub-individuality. But in reading great

literature I become a thousand men and yet remain myself. Like the night sky in the Greek poem, I see with a myriad eyes, but it is still I who see. Here, as in worship, in love, in moral action, and in knowing, I transcend myself; and am never more myself than when I do.

A large self, yet obedient and willing to surrender, neither imperial nor woefully pained—just quiet. At worship at Trinity Church in Headington, close to their home in Headington Quarry, the Lewis brothers were very private, according to the vicar, the Reverend R. E. Head. He told me "They always sat in the same place and were always out first. Others never noticed them."

I

When in his prime in the 1940s and when it was his practice to have students, friends, and colleagues to dinner parties at Magdalen College, Oxford, at which much drinking and even more revelry would transpire, Lewis might perform an astonishing parlor trick. Upon being told how terrible it was to remember nothing, Lewis would reply that it was worse to forget nothing, as was the case with everything he read. Of course, this declaration would be met with incredulity and demands that he put up or shut up. And so he would solicit a series of numbers from the most skeptical guest, these corresponding to a bookcase, a shelf within that case, and a book upon that shelf. The guest would then fetch the specified volume, which could be in any of several languages, open to a page of his own choosing, read aloud from that page, and stop where he pleased. Lewis would then quote the rest of that page from memory. To the pleasure of all present he would, as John Wain saw, show off.

Playing tricks and showing off was just the sort of thing that amused and attracted some of his audiences and antagonized most of his critics. It was the sort of thing they claimed he did in his books and talks. Of course, both praise and blame were functions of his rising reputation from the early 1930s to the late 1940s, especially during the war years, closely following upon *The Screwtape Letters* (virtually a publishing phenomenon), the BBC radio broadcasts, *The Broadcast Talks*, and other books based upon the BBC series. It is difficult now to appreciate the magnitude of Lewis's impact; but, combined with his firmly-established credential as a prominent university figure, his *auctoritee*, as it would have been called in the Middle Ages, it was very great and much resented. Of course, that he held opinions disturbing to opinion-makers, especially highbrow literary and theological opinion-makers, eschewed euphemism and inconclusiveness, and spoke "out of license"— not only was he a layman but a professor, for whom such direct, common, and wide appeal was, well, in bad taste—only augmented the resentment. The degree of his fame is especially striking when one considers that *The Chronicles of Narnia, Surprised by Joy*, the massive volume of literary history, *The Four Loves, Till We Have Faces, Reflections on the Psalms*, and a short shelf-full of others, had yet to be written.

In the second paragraph of *The Everlasting Man*, G. K. Chesterton describes the critics of Christianity in his typically paradoxical way, by telling us that they have not really escaped it: "They are doubtful of their very doubts. Their criticism has taken on a curious tone; as of a random and illiterate heckling." Just so do many of Lewis's critics sound today. One theological liberal charged in 1946 that Lewis was "simply using the church as an excuse for his dreary attacks on everything he hasn't bothered to understand" and that he had done "a grave disservice to European civilization" in his radio talks. In its review of *The Case for Christianity*, the *New York Herald Tribune* (1943) called Lewis's statement of Christian theology "almost incredibly naïve" and as evidence merely cited—with no further argument, as though their summary spoke for itself—his having adduced the Fall, Satan, the Incarnation, the Resurrection, the doctrine of Atonement, and the Christian belief in the Second Coming, that is, Mere Christianity. Famously, Alistair Cooke, in the *New Republic* (1944), wrote that "the personal values of several million Britons and Americans stand in imminent danger of befuddlement at which Mr. Lewis is so transparently adroit." Norman Pittinger, even more famously because of his stature and because Lewis chose to answer him, called him, in 1958, "a dangerous apologist and an inept theologian."

Others, with their long-simmering antagonism apparently beyond their control, attacked Lewis posthumously when they were supposed to be reviewing the Hooper-Green biography. John Carey, in the *New Statesman* (July 5, 1974), complained that I. A. Richards and F. R. Leavis, two Lewis adversaries, never entered tutorial discussions. He concluded that Lewis was marked by "blindness, prejudice, and sheer bull-necked stupidity." In the *Guardian* (July 11, 1974), Martin Jarret-Ker dismissed Lewis as "merely a 'Greats' man who never got beyond Plato." Perhaps John Raymond, in the Sunday *Times* (July 14, 1974) made the oddest attack of all when he attributed to others what he would not claim for himself: "There are those who also thought . . . that his theology . . . stank of logic."

Most reviewers of that first biography, however, praised Lewis. One called him "a born communicator"; another, a justifiable "legend in his own lifetime"; a third, "a splendid philosophy tutor" who "recognizably outclass[ed] us intellectually"—"combative," "ebullient," and "witty." John Barley in the *Times Literary Supplement* (July 12, 1974) also noted Lewis's combativeness and vindicated his claim as an Old Western Man, writing that Lewis provoked controversy by invoking "a world gone by," that he was so much of the past, in fact, that "he became new with insights"; that he stood for mere Christianity and scholarship "just as a horse stands for horseliness"; and that all along he was quite innocent of his accomplishments. But the most telling praise came from the redoubtable Malcolm Muggeridge, who noted Lewis's sheer goodness and personal sanctity, "in his innermost being. His teaching and his writing were his *opus dei*."

Over the decades there have been many others who have attacked Lewis in a variety of ways. Assaults on his arguments he would have, as he did during his lifetime, welcomed. He did respond to Pittinger by saying that if a century earlier others had done what he had there would have been no need for him and, in a legendary episode, revised the third chapter of *Miracles* because he thought he had been seriously bested at the Socratic Club by Elizabeth Anscombe, who would her self become a very great philosopher. He never responded to *ad hominem* attacks, those for example by Kathleen Nott in *The Emperor's Clothes* (1953). He just might have responded to David Holbrook ("The Problem of C. S. Lewis" in *Children's Literature in Education*, 1973) with a punch in the nose: Holbrook apparently did not learn in the schoolyard that one is careful when discussing another man's mother—dead mother, at that.

Reviews and attacks were not joined by serious study of Lewis's work until Chad Walsh published the very first book on him, *C. S. Lewis: Apostle to the Skeptics*, in 1949, one year after the completion of the first doctoral dissertation, "The

Theology of C. S. Lewis," by Edgar Boss. But some dozen years would pass before additional systematic work was produced, beginning with Dabney Hart's doctoral dissertation, "C. S. Lewis's Defense of Poesie." And not until after Lewis's death would the tide of serious interest turn towards Lewis, punctuated most notable by Clyde Kilby's *The Christian World of C. S. Lewis*. Since then the flow of work has come in waves, always with the most recent wave cresting higher than its predecessor. Many of these studies have sought to systematize or reformulate Lewis's work, with varying success. But the impulse is understandable—precisely because Lewis was unsystematic and never wrote his own *summa*. And of course it has proven as tempting for authors to introduce Lewis to new generations of readers as it has for magazines to issue retrospectives on his life and work.

Generally, I think the most useful studies have been the most recent, especially those, usually in essays variously collected, that place Lewis in context and otherwise explore the roots of his thinking. A fine example of such work is Jared C. Lobdell's "C. S. Lewis's Ransom Stories and Their Eighteenth-Century Ancestry" in Schakel and Huttar's *Word and Story in C. S. Lewis*. Though he overextends his argument, Lobdell is convincing in his claim that eighteenth-century literature, particularly Swift's *Gulliver's Travels* and Dr. Johnson's *Rasselas*, accounts for the "certain[ty] that the business of philosophy was, in Lewis's mind, very much mixed in with the business of fiction." On the other hand, Lewis was wary of the scholar's habit of searching out "influences." Too frequently "influence" is sloppily used, salient distinctions left unmade, and bad reasoning generated from bad evidence. In such essays as "The Genesis of a Medieval Book," "On Criticism," and "The Literary Impact of the Authorized Version," he distinguishes between a source, which provides matter, and an influence, which bears upon manner. And there are various kinds of influence, too, with the fullest sort being the least self-consciously arrayed. A mind might be stamped by an influence and not know it, so a critic's inference is a tenuous one. In Lewis's own case we have been told explicitly of several influences, including MacDonald, Boehme, Chesterton, and Alexander; David Lindsay, Charles Williams, E. Nesbitt, and Kenneth Grahame, among others.

Almost certainly Lewis never read what Chesterton had to say about fairy tales in the *Illustrated London News* (December 2, 1905); at least there is no evidence of such a reading. Even if he had, the influence would not have been "apologetic," strictly speaking. But Chesterton's view is a fine example of how the cast of one man's mind can be reflected in that of another, even absent a direct source. Besides, the passage is compelling *per se*:

> Fairy-tales are as normal as milk or bread. Civilization changes [we would hear an echo of this in Lewis]; but fairy-tales never change. Some of the details of the fairy-tale may seem odd to us; but its spirit is the spirit of folk-lore; and folk-lore is, in strict translation, the German for common sense.... *The fairy tale is full of mental health* [emphasis added].... A seven-headed dragon is, perhaps, a terrifying monster, but a child who has never heard about him [Eustace, of *The Voyage of the Dawn Treader*?] is a much more terrifying monster than he is. The maddest griffin or chimera is not so wild a supposition as a school without fairy-tales.

With respect to apologetic influences, however, we must infer, for with the exceptions of the monumental MacDonald

and the sixteenth-century Richard Hooker, praise of whom
must still count as only circumstantial evidence, Lewis rarely
attributes. He does cite Chesterton as an intellectual but not
a rhetorical influence. If one did not know better, one might
mistake snippets of *The Everlasting Man* (1925), for example,
for Lewis's writing—topics, lines of argument, tone, stylistic
devices are that similar; but they would have to be snippets,
for Chesterton is far more ruminative than Lewis, who argues
at the bone. Here is the beginning of Chesterton's pivotal work:

> There are two ways of getting home; and one of them is
> to stay there. [Lewis's affection for home, a Home, is stead-
> fast in his work.] The other is to walk around the whole
> world till we come back to the same place. [Not unlike
> John the Pilgrim? Chesterton then refers to a book he
> never wrote, "by far the best book I have ever written,"
> which he proceeds to summarize.] . . . It concerned some
> boy whose farm or cottage stood on such a slope, and
> who went on his travels to find something . . . and when
> he was far enough from home he looked back and saw
> that his own farm and kitchen-garden shining flat on the
> hillside like the colouring and quarterings of a shield, were
> but parts of some such gigantic figure, but which was too
> large and too close to be seen. That, I think, is a true
> picture of the progress of any really *independent* [em-
> phasis added] intelligence today; and that is the point of
> this book.

Near the end of the book, in his first of two appendices,
Chesterton refers back to his mention of a Cro-Magnon skull
"that was much larger and finer than a modern skull." Apparently an evolutionist had warned against "anything being
inferred from one specimen." Chesterton concludes with an
idea and in a tone that Lewis would echo: "It is the duty of a

solitary skull to prove that our fathers were our inferiors. Any solitary skull presuming to prove that they were superior is felt to be suffering from a swelled head."

II

In his introduction to a translation of St. Athanasius's *De Incarnatione Verbum Dei*, as we have seen, Lewis notes that St. Athanasius opposes compromise religions in favor of "central Christianity ('mere Christianity' as Baxter called it)"; he welcomes his author's approach to miracles, "which is badly needed today, for it is the final answer to those who object to them as 'arbitrary and meaningless violations of the laws of Nature'." In particular, Lewis admires a book that inspires devotion by being doctrinal. To note the date of this introduction, 1944, is to note that most of his output of non-devotional books was to follow within not too many years, especially *Miracles* and, a bit later, *Reflections on the Psalms*, which is semi-devotional and crypto-doctrinal. But St. Athanasius was surely an influence as well as a source. His combative stance, popular tone, direct address to the audience, use of such engaging figures of thought as invented dialogue and interrogation, and, above all, his use of striking analogies all found their way into Lewis's apologetics:

> Everyone is by nature afraid of death and of bodily dissolution; the marvel of marvels is that he who is enfolded in the faith of the cross despises this natural fear and for the sake of the cross is no longer cowardly in face of it. The natural property of fire is to burn. Suppose, then, that there was a substance such as the Indian asbestos is said to be, which had no fear of being burnt, but rather displayed the impotence of the fire by proving itself

unburnable. If anyone doubted the truth of this, all he need do would be to wrap himself up in the substance in question and then touch the fire.

In this same introduction Lewis cites William Law as a lion in the path of an atheist; even "in the urbane sobriety of the eighteenth century one was not safe." Law had a controversial career, yet his *A Serious Call to a Devout and Holy Life* (1728) was one of the great best-sellers of the century. Though its tone is militant to the point of being strident and is far more hortatory than anything of Lewis's, it had a very great impact on its ordinary readers. Law referred to their common practices—practices they would have recognized—and told them, without ever resorting to fear-appeals, a thorough conversion is necessary. God simply cannot allow a little bit of Hell in Heaven, as Lewis would so dramatically depict in *The Great Divorce*. The most efficacious instrument commonly available to the Christian for sustaining his faith is prayer, which is best if varied and done in private. Lewis says the same thing in *Letters to Malcolm: Chiefly on Prayer*. But the rhetorical lesson learned from St. Athanasius and from Law was the same: adapt to the audience of the age and address them directly.

Perhaps best of all Lewis used (as he loved) Richard Hooker, whose *Laws of Ecclesiastical Polity* (1593, 1597, 1648, 1662; respectively, books I-IV, V, VI and VIII, VII) is both source and influence. Lewis appreciated Hooker's unwillingness to join party or denomination at the expense of truth, for the universe is much more complex than doctrinal differences would allow. He even goes so far as to redeem Papists, "in this way and others going far beyond the limits of personal or controversial prudence." Although Hooker's ecclesiology leaves the Church relatively free of scripture and dependent, though not slavishly, upon tradition, he eschews as irrelevant the issues fought over by different sects. To live by absolute secular authority is a gross blunder, for the "'law rational,' which men commonly used to call the Law of Nature—the 'Light of Reason',—should prevail." Lewis declared that "The most important value of Hooker's work lies in his defence of that light."

It is a defense of that light which constitutes Lewis's least classifiable, most purely philosophical book, *The Abolition of Man.* "The main principles of reason are in themselves apparent," wrote Hooker, "for to make nothing evident of itself unto man's understanding were to take away all possibility of knowing anything. And herein that of Theophrastus is true, 'They that seek a reason of all things do utterly overthrow reason'." Lewis would argue precisely along these lines, saying that the law of nature is practical reason itself, neither demanding nor admitting of proof, that an *ought* must not be dismissed because it cannot produce some *is* as its credential; for if nothing is self-evident, nothing can be proved. "To 'see through' all things is the same as not to see." The opinions which Lewis chooses to praise are the opinions he came himself to hold: all good things are of God, who is "unspeakably tran scendent; but also unspeakably immanent"; we "glorify God in all actions"; "divine testimony" and "demonstrative reasoning are equally infallible"; equality is not inherently preferable; and so on. But in addition to the opinions, a great value of the *Polity* is that it

> marks a revolution in the art of controversy. . . . Truths unfold themselves, quietly and in due order. . . . He writes of Man, if fallen, "yet now redeemed and already partially glorified," of Man in communion with all faithful men, because "nature doth presume that how many men there are in the world, so many gods as it were there are." We hope, hereafter, to "live as it were the life of God". And

all of this is in a style, for its purpose, perhaps the most perfect in English; removed from the colloquial, not decorated, yet often rendered in the "voice of the people" . . . his often mischievous humor is always part of the argumentative context. And much of his argument is on behalf of moderation in controversy, while everywhere in his writing there is a sense of "the beautiful variety of all things".

If St. Athanasius provided Lewis with a manual, then Hooker became his apologetic sunbeam.

Literary sources and influences, as we see even with an argument as learned and well-constructed as Lobdell's, are difficult to argue for or—even when attested to by Lewis himself—to understand. In the case of E. R. Eddison's *The Worm Ouroboros*, Lewis's enthusiasm is hard to fathom. There is nothing numinous about it, the narrative is unwieldy, the style inconsistent, and the satisfactions of adventure and character intermittent; but I hasten to add that the book has won great praise from many notables other than Lewis. Different? Maybe. "Other"? Certainly not: It lacks even the lineaments of the sort of fantasy that would nourish Lewis's deepest imaginative roots, such as those in Morris's *The Well at the World's End*. In "Imagination Baptized, or, 'Holiness' in the *Chronicles of Narnia*" (in Schakel, *The Longing for a Form*), Eliane Tixier reflects Lewis's own assessment of Morris's book: Ultimately the hero, Ralph, having answered a call to journey forth and found the Well, chooses not to dwell in the World's End and returns instead to the world. But the lure of Joy is there through the husk of Morris's mannered language and heavy narrative; and the final Book is "The Road Home." Notwithstanding weaknesses of execution, Joy and home—especially a return home—are all Lewis would have needed to be transported.

E. Nesbitt moved, though not quite transported, him in her stories of the Bastable children, especially in *The Treasure-Seekers*. Her jumping about from one world to another (in her case, from present to past), a secret shared by children alone; the presence of strange creatures; the involvement of a knowing, but not-quite-safe adult; the attitude of occasional direct address and its concomitant self-conscious story-telling stance; and the manners and customs of late Victorian and Edwardian England all found their way into *The Chronicles of Narnia*. But the book that tripped the imaginative and spiritual wires was surely Kenneth Grahame's *The Wind in the Willows*. Whose internal landscape would not be permanently altered by Mole and Rat's vision in chapter seven, the very title of which, "The Piper at the Gates of Dawn," compels even the hyperkinetic reader to be still and hush? The chapter begins and builds slowly, the mystery deepening, the response quickening, until the very souls of Rat and Mole have been quieted and finely tuned:

> Then suddenly the Mole felt a great Awe fall upon him, an awe that turned his muscles to water, bowed his head, and rooted his feet to the ground . . . he felt wonderfully at peace and happy . . . [and] knew it could only mean that some august Presence was near. . . . And still there was utter silence in the populous bird-haunted branches around them; and still the light grew and grew. Perhaps he would never have dared to raise his eyes, but that . . . the call seemed still dominant and imperious. He might not refuse, were Death himself waiting to strike him instantly. . . . Trembling he obeyed, and raised his humble head; and then, in that utter clearness of the imminent dawn, while Nature, flushed with fullness of incredible colour, seemed to hold her breath for the event, he looked

into the very eyes of the Friend and Helper . . . and still,
as he looked, he lived, and still, as he lived, he wondered.
"Rat!" he found breath to whisper, shaking. "Are you
afraid?" "Afraid!" murmured the Rat, his eyes shining
with unutterable love. "Afraid! Of *Him*? O, never, never!
And yet—and yet—O, Mole, I am afraid!" Then the two
animals, crouching to the earth, bowed their heads and
did worship.

Grahame had not read Bevan's *Symbolism and Belief*, but Lewis
read both. The latter helped him to think, write, and perhaps
believe; but the former helped him to recognize, know, and
heal, for to read Grahame is "to grow in mental health."

Two other authors are indisputably both influences and
sources: Charles Williams and David Lindsay. Of the first I
can add nothing to what has already been said by Lewis himself
and by others, all of which is most ably summarized by Brian
Horne in "A Peculiar Debt: The Influence of Charles Williams
on C. S. Lewis" in Walker and Patrick's *A Christian for All
Christians*. Horne is especially strong at showing the implicit
possibilities of influence that may have marked *The Screwtape
Letters*, *Till We Have Faces* (which Horne unfortunately calls
"allegorical"), and *Letters to Malcolm*. Notwithstanding Lewis's
description of Williams's death in 1945 as the "greatest loss"
he had ever known, he claimed that he never consciously
imitated Williams, although he admits that he may have done
so unconsciously. Nevertheless, we have Nevill Coghill telling us that Lewis learned his thinking only from Williams and
Tolkien; and Austin Farrer adds, "His debts in personal wisdom and literary inspiration to his wife and to Charles Williams were visible to all." A more skeptical view than Horne's,
shared by Tolkien, is expressed by Humphrey Carpenter in his
The Inklings.

David Lindsay's *A Voyage to Arcturus* (1920) is not only continually praised by Lewis but proclaimed as both a source and an influence. What so drew Lewis was not its writing, which is as weak as he said it is, but its flavor, its "adjectival quality," as he might have put it. The landscape of the planet Tormance is odd, dramatic, unpredictable, severe, and sometimes internally inconsistent. In short, it is a "spiritual landscape," as Lewis called it, as is the conflict, engaged by forces of what Lindsay regards as utter Good and utter Evil: Lindsay's near-diabolical metaphysics are not merely Manichaean but duplicitous as well. And he provides one of the elements so prized by Lewis and evident in all his fiction, the hero Maskull's "lived dialectic," with all its necessary errors. So impressed was Lewis's imagination by Lindsay's work that *Out of the Silent Planet* and *Perelandra* virtually recapitulate the flavor of Tormance as well as the adventure of spiritual discovery; in fact, its very landscape shows up in Lewis's books. It also seems likely that the aborted *Dark Tower*—its opening, ugly sensuality, and ambivalent hero, as well as the very tower—was directly inspired by it.

A concrete source from *Arcturus* occurs near the end, when Lindsay describes the dreaded absorption process and its effect on individuality: "What had been fiery spirit but a moment ago, was now a disgusting mass of crawling, wriggling individuals, each whirl of pleasure-seeking will having, as a nucleus, a fragmentary spark of living green fire. . . . The individual whirls were jostling with, even devouring, each other." Echoes of this passage are in the horrific Un-man of *Perelandra* and in *Screwtape*, including "Screwtape proposes a toast." In what surely is an inversion of the Christian concept of the Body of Christ—I would call it parody but for Lindsay's utter lack of satirical intent—we are told how the "spirit-stream . . . was not below individuality, but above it," thus divinizing the Devil, precisely what Lewis reversed in *Screwtape*. Then Lindsay concludes: "During those moments of anguish, all thoughts of the self—the corruption of his life on earth—were scorched out of Nightspore's soul . . . perhaps not for the first time. . . . 'Are you not Surtur [a *benevolent* god for Lindsay], Krag?' 'Yes.' 'Yes,' said Nightspore [who is Maskull] in a slow voice, without surprise. 'But what is your name on earth?' 'It is pain.' 'That, too, I must have known'."

Lewis would not have been surprised, either psychologically or artistically; his alchemical imagination would transmute anything it and his intellect had retained if the transmutation would serve his end. I do not mean to suggest that Lewis was "derivative" in the sense that term is ordinarily used. And he never set out, as far as most can see, to copy an author or to re-tell someone else's tale, not even in *Till We Have Faces*, coyly subtitled "A Myth Re-Told." He was simply as unoriginal as he claimed all along—unoriginal here and there, sometimes in manner, other times in matter. But his syntheses are freshness itself, and he could write vastly better than almost any of his sources and influences. Perhaps without Anstey, Beatrix Potter, Nesbitt, Kenneth Grahame, and others, there would be no Narnia as we know it; without Wells and Lindsay, no Space trilogy; without St. Athanasius, William Law, and George MacDonald no *Great Divorce* or *Mere Christianity*. But we may as well say that without the eighteenth century there would have been no *Screwtape Letters*, or without the Middle Ages no *Pilgrim's Regress*. Lewis made others his own, as he did entire genres and whole traditions. That is among the reasons why he is a man of letters of surpassing *auctoritee*.

III

In reviewing Alfred Kazin's *God and the American Writer* for *National Review*, Jeffrey Hart wrote the following (December 8, 1997): "The Protestant principle, as Matthew Arnold said, is individual judgment. The exercising of individual judgments led first to great religious fissures, then to the multiplication of sects, and finally to the ultimate sect—that is, the individual human being on his own; at once the preacher and the congregation, who allows himself to be overheard by an audience outside his sect of one. . . . It is not surprising that the sect of one produced extraordinary garrulousness." This is an overstatement, of course, and as much a description of intellectual independence and Lewis's need for "primary" experience as of intellectual vanity. But its error rests in its degree. Greatly modulated by Mere Christianity, it applies manifestly to Lewis, who suggested as much about himself in writing about the diabolical Screwtape: "Some have paid me an undeserved compliment by supposing that my *Letters* were the ripe fruit of many years' study in moral and ascetic theology. They forgot that there is an equally reliable, though less creditable, way of learning how temptation works. 'My heart'—I need no other's —'sheweth me the wickedness of the ungodly'."

Independence, eclecticism, and an allegiance to individual, primary experience in part may account for the fact that Lewis never wrote a systematic treatise on social theory, ethics, philosophy, or even theology. Intellectual systems are artificial, removed from the objects they order, and, because they become hypostatized, necessarily false. Only with regard to literature did he hold any theories; but with respect to the broadest of these, the nature of literature and its function, the theory was not "his," not new, and not elaborately stated, be-

ing, in the first place, more a description of the healthy relationship of reader to book than a theory. Just so with thought
and experience, a different sort of text, but one which, like any
other, invites interpretation. Theoryless, Lewis submitted
himself to the text on its own terms, naturally becoming its
critic. He had contempt for such books as *Literary Taste and
How to Form It*, as though taste should mediate the genuine
literary experience and be learned "like golf." When he became a prominent adversary of F. R. Leavis, the great highbrow, exclusionary judge of "serious" literature, he would insist
that learning requires freedom for students, who need only to
be led by "older students," not dictated to by schoolmasters,
as though having their noses blown for them by nurses. Such
was the pattern of Lewis's intellectual genius and of the philosophical aspect of his conversion and its immediate aftermath.

It hardly need be said that the absence of a system does
not imply the absence of intellectual order; even if the imaginative man was older in him than the analytical man, Lewis
could produce, within two years of his conversion, *The Pilgrim's
Regress: An Allegorical Apology for Christianity, Reason and Romanticism*, a relentlessly analytical, systematic allegory. Its
importance is that it shows us how absolute, decisive, utterly
thorough, and preternaturally fast was Lewis's mind and that
it comes very near to being an exemplar of the thirty-year cor-
pus that was to follow. (It is also his second autobiographical
work, the first being *Dymer*.) Though never out of print this
book is not one of Lewis's more popular ones: it is esoteric
and because of its allegorical mode formally alien to our
modern sensibility. It is not, as some have claimed, dated in
the dragons it seeks to slay; rather, its emphases seem inap-
propriate. The objects of Lewis's attack seem real to most of
us but less salient than they did to the author. The response

of Jane Spence Southron, writing in the *New York Times Book Review* (December 8, 1935), provides an interesting counterpoint to the more current view:

> A modern man's intricate journey . . . and the highly complex mental processes that distinguish him from creatures of a different order are resolved, here, into the utmost simplicity. . . . He is . . . an intellectual of our own day, who is not content to take anything in life at its face value *and* who makes use of the stored-up knowledge of the past and the possibilities of practical adventures in living to help him in his explorations. . . . On its literary side the book deserves high rating. The allegorical characters are not just abstractions but objectively real and subjectively true to their inner meaning. The language, throughout, is plain, straightforward and leanly significant.

It is also taut, self-contained and, he would come to say, of an "uncharitable temper."

Its first enduring feature is its deceptively simple plot. (Most of Lewis's plots are deceptively simple, with the exception of *That Hideous Strength*, the third book of his Space trilogy.) John-the-Pilgrim flees Puritania, ruled by an ostensibly cruel landlord in the habit of unexpectedly foreclosing on his tenants' leases, to seek the object of his sweet, yet painful, desire— a remote Western Island. Guided by Virtue, John attempts to keep to the narrow road, but he is distracted both to the north and to the south. Finally, he reaches the forbidding chasm of *Peccatum Adae*; weary and wounded, his clothes in tatters, he almost despairs, but old Mother Kirk (herself nearly decrepit) describes to him a perilous path descending into and then crossing the canyon. Though John tries valiantly to make the climb, he is overcome by fear and fatigue and stops, desperate, huddled on a ledge. Wisdom, Philosophy, and History have

proved as useless to him as the Brown Girls (sexual temptation), Sigismund Enlightenment (Freudianism), the Giant (our
zeitgeist), Savage (nihilism, served by either black or red
dwarfs—totalitarians of the left and of the right), and others
with whom he has contended.

Out of the dark comes a voice promising safety at the price
of absolute trust. Though frightened, John accepts the offer
and is easily led to the bottom of the canyon, where he bathes
in a pool. When he emerges he sees the man whose voice he
heard and is incredulous, for he had come to believe that stories
of a god descending to earth and then rising to the profit,
somehow, of humans were nothing but pagan myths. It is then
that Christ explains myth to John. Baptized, he rises to the
other side of the chasm, sees that the Island is close to his place
of origin, and returns. On the journey home he sees the same
world differently than he did when first he traveled the road:
Mother Kirk, for example, is vibrant and glorious, and the
South—far from being a fertile and opulent tropics—is actually a burning swamp. Acknowledging that the world and
all that is in it is a fallen copy of what is meant to be, John
resolves to lead a Christian life, now possessed of a faith in
the redemption of the world and of himself.

The story closely parallels the one told in *Surprised by Joy*
(the third, and formal, autobiography). The absoluteness of
categories, the wholeness of experience and its meaningful-
ness, the reliability of reason, the epistemological validity of
myth and metaphor—these and other elements constitute the
lineaments of Lewis's thought; these, and Joy:

> But what I meant by "Romanticism" when I wrote the
> *Pilgrim's Regress* and what I would still be taken to mean
> on the title page of this book was a particular recurrent
> experience which dominated my childhood and adoles-

cence and which I hastily called "Romantic" because inanimate nature and marvellous literature were among the things that evoked it. I still believe that the experience is common, commonly misunderstood and of immense importance, but I know now that in other minds it arises under other *stimuli* and is entangled with other irrelevancies.

Before converting, Lewis had to learn how to know, to see, to trust what he was, and to interpret. Is access to Joy limited to a study of the tracks left behind? If so, are we not simply gazing upon ourselves, introspecting under the guise of outwardly exploring and thus mistaking the desire for its object? If, however, Otherness *per se*—the very wellspring of Joy, after all—might be apprehended, then by what route do we approach it? Under what conditions? And guided by the light of what faculty? The very fact that answers exist at all lends credence to the objective reliability of Otherness. After all, if there are road signs, then there must be roads; and if roads, then perhaps a single place towards which they run. "The dialectic . . . faithfully followed would retrieve all mistakes, head you off from all false paths, and force you not to propound, but to live through, a sort of ontological proof"—a lived "dialectic of desire." Lewis's literary experiences had already demonstrated the efficacy of forgetting the self for the sake of delighting in the qualities of worlds other than the one he occupied; now he would discern the lineaments of meaning in the larger text of experience, Inner, Outer, and Otherwise.

For Lewis philosophy was never merely the history of ideas or, as the fashion would soon become, especially at Cambridge, the study of language for its own sake. Instead, Lewis had learned from Kant the distinction between the Noumenal and the Phenomenal self, the difference between "a fully conscious

'I' whose connections with the 'me' of introspection were loose
and transitory." About real objects, that Phenomenal self could
have real feelings; and if there were real feelings, then must
there not be real objects? Discovering the true nature of those
objects—or Object—is, of course, the story of Lewis becoming first a Theist and then a Christian. The real breakthrough
was the discovery of meaning in experience—internal and
external, literary, emotional, intellectual, and sensory. Lewis
was concerned with no less a question than reality—and that
question most assuredly includes the self, in this case construed
as mind. The two philosophers who early were most useful
to him were Bishop Berkeley (1685-1753) and David Hume
(1711-76), who had raised in Lewis's mind a central question
regarding introspection: Is it not a question-begging process?
Are not the subject and object the same, to the exclusion of
any referent outside of the self which had been the object of
thinking and about which we believed we might learn more
if only we back-tracked along the original thought-process?

About Berkeley's subjective idealism, which held that only
minds are real, that one great mind created other, independent minds, and that what we take as reality is in fact the ideas
that these minds have, Lewis noted in a book of lecture notes
he called *Thickening* (1924) that "to ask 'what is in my mind
while I am thinking?' usually means to stop the real thinking
and then 'introspect': and then I could naturally find only the
irrelevant pictures or words which, as a matter of psychological
fact, do accompany the thinking. . . . Does all introspection
always leave out the important things?" Months thereafter he
was accusing Hume, who would turn the tables on Berkeley
by attacking both rationalism and natural theology, of falling "into the same fallacy of 'introspection' as Berkeley." In
other words, mental self-regard leads to mere solipsism? Hence

the importance of his strong and enduring belief: "It is more important that Heaven should exist than that any of us should reach it." The first step is to establish that omissions are "important things." Lewis was highly responsive to literature and to nature (especially to the Castlereagh Hills, that early medium of Joy), both of which seemed to beckon with real and objective qualities; but this responsiveness was "romantic," consisting chiefly of a taste for the exotic, and he does not encounter a "baptized" nature until he reads Wordsworth in his late teens.

It was for his friend Arthur to broaden the horizon of important things by teaching his friend to *lower* his gaze:

> In literature he influenced me more, or more permanently, than I did him. He . . . had another taste which I lacked till I met him and with which, to my great good, he infected me for life; this was the taste for what he called "the good, solid, old books". . . . Under Arthur's influence I read at this time all the best Waverleys, all the Brontes, and all the Jane Austens. . . . The very qualities which had previously deterred me from such books Arthur taught me to see as their charm. What I would have called their "stodginess" or "ordinariness" he called "Homeliness"—a key word in his imagination—the rooted quality which attaches them to all our simple experiences, to weather, food, the family, the neighborhood. . . . And in his search for the homely he taught me to see other things as well. But for him I should never have known the beauty of the ordinary vegetables that we destine to the pot. "Drills," he used to say. "Just ordinary drills of cabbages—what can be better?". . . . Often he recalled my eyes from the horizon just to look through a hole in a hedge, to see nothing more than a farmyard in its midmorning solitude, and perhaps a gray

cat squeezing its way under a barn door, or a bent old woman with a wrinkled, motherly face coming back with an empty bucket from the pigsty. But best of all we liked it when the Homely and the unhomely met in sharp juxtaposition, when some shivering quarry pool under a moon-rise could be seen on our left, and on our right the smoking chimney and lamplit window of a cottage that was just settling down for the night.

IV

With heightened perception came altered valuation, as objects began to be simply themselves, possessed of an integrity independent of the effect they produced. Lewis would learn to revel in concreteness:

> A. K. Hamilton Jenkin . . . continued [what Arthur had begun] my education as a seeing, listening, smelling, receptive creature. Arthur had had his preference for the Homely. But Jenkin seemed to be able to enjoy everything; even ugliness. I learned from him that we should attempt a total surrender to whatever atmosphere was offering itself at the moment; in a squalid town to seek out those very places where its squalor rose to grimness and almost grandeur, on a dismal day to find the most dismal and dripping wood, on a windy day to seek the windiest ridge . . . a serious, yet gleeful, determination to rub one's nose in the very quiddity of each thing, to rejoice in its being (so magnificently) what it was.

It is no wonder that Lewis responded readily to Samuel Alexander's *Space, Time and Deity,* which confirmed the concreteness of things by establishing coherence as a rationale for integrity and by requiring that concreteness be a quality possessed by other objects, rather than a quality brought to them by the mind. Introspection is the suspension of normal modes of thought, so it encounters mainly mental images and physical sensations when it searches for, say, Joy: "The great error is to mistake this mere sediment or track or byproduct for the activities themselves." Alexander showed that mental categories are fundamental properties of Space-Time: things are not true and false of themselves, but real regarding their own coherence. This version of *quiddity* had to stimulate Lewis, especially when the thing whose "thingness" cohered so strongly suggests Joy: "The religious emotion is as unique and self-sufficient as hungry appetite or love. . . . There is in fact no duty to be religious anymore than there is a duty to be hungry. . . . It is in our constitution."

This ontological expedition requires a reliable course along which the Noumenal self might travel, and it is precisely here that Lewis acknowledges his greatest debt to Alexander, whose technical distinction between "Enjoyment" and "Contemplation" would become "an indispensable tool of thought":

> When you see a table you "enjoy" the act of seeing and "contemplate" the table. In bereavement you contemplate the beloved and the beloved's death and, in Alexander's sense, "enjoy" the loneliness and grief; but a psychologist, if he were considering you as a case of melancholia, would be contemplating your grief and enjoying psychology. . . . When we think a thought, "thought" is a cognate accusative (like "blow" in "strike a blow"). We enjoy the thought . . . and, in so doing, contemplate the object of thought. . . . In other words the enjoyment and contemplation of our inner activities are incompatible. . . . all introspection is in one respect misleading.

Thus all the value of any object lies in the contemplation of

that object for its own sake, not in the contemplation of our
own enjoyment of it. So "in deepest solitude there is a road
right out of the self, a commerce with something which, by
refusing to identify itself with . . . any state of our own minds,
proclaims itself sheerly objective." "Enjoyment" of, say, myth
and "contemplation" of the source of the myth must be two
aspects of one transcendent faculty. "Thinking transcends the
distinction of subject and object. . . ." That is, if thought is
valid it cannot be part of nature, purely material. "Mind [is]
no late-come epiphenomenon; the whole universe is, in the
last resort, mental; . . . our logic [is] participation in a cos-
mic Logos." We are prohibited, then, from "contemplating"
our "enjoyment" in any meaningful way. At the end of his book,
Alexander clearly argues that we are being moved along that
road (by God) toward deity, and that religion is the realization of this movement. "The form of the desired is in the desire": In short, a rationale for the Joy Lewis had known as that
small Irish boy. In "enjoying," and in attempting to get others to "enjoy," Lewis could *not* have written a systematic treatise on theology. Not idly did he remind his readers that he
was no systematic theologian.

During this time the long Great War with Owen Barfield
was coming to a close. Although Anthroposophy was mostly
about the relationship of language to the imagination, Lewis
had to fight through its layers of spiritualism, occultism, and
some mysticism, all inherent in Steiner's philosophy and earnestly pursued and adopted in serious and well-regarded works
by Barfield. Lewis's final epistemological position probably
would have prevailed even had there been no Great War. Astral
events, clairvoyance, and psychic forces were rejected as unnecessary to final conviction—and as an unhealthy, ultimately
gnostic, exaltation of the self. The concept would be of con-

tinuing concern. Recall for a moment Barfield's observation that Lewis willed his own self-disregard and then consider this retrospective declaration of purpose: "I have wanted to . . . expel that quite unchristian worship of the human individual as such which is so rampant. . . . I mean the pestilent notion that each of us starts with a treasure called 'Personality' . . . and that to expand and express this. . . is the main end of life." This theme of self-centeredness, its dangers, and of course its antidotes lie at the center of Lewis's philosophy of human nature.

Once he accomplished the expulsion upon himself—"You can't study people," he said, "you can only get to know them," finally including himself—the inevitable beckoned to this most willful anarchist. While riding atop a bus on the way home Lewis was offered a "wholly free choice." He became aware that he was holding something at bay, or shutting something out, and that he "could open the door or keep it shut." He knew that to open the door "meant the incalculable, but neither choice was presented as a duty." He chose to open. "I say, I chose, yet it did not really seem possible to do the opposite. On the other hand, I was aware of no motives. You could argue that I was not a free agent, but I am more inclined to think that this came nearer to being a perfectly free act than most that I have ever done. Necessity may not be the opposite of freedom, and perhaps a man is most free when, instead of producing motives, he could only say, 'I am what I do'. . . . Enough had been thought, and said, and felt, and imagined. It was about time that something should be done."

When James Stephens's Philosopher in *The Crock of Gold* sallied forth to regain his neighbor's daughter, lured away by Pan to avenge the theft of the Leprechaun's crock of gold, he too found that something should be done, for he was being left no choice:

[H]is opinions were undergoing a curious change. Right and wrong were meeting and blending together so closely that it became difficult to dissever them, and the obloquy attaching to the one seemed out of proportion altogether to its importance, while the other by no means justified the eulogy wherewith it was connected. Was there any immediate, or even distant, effect on life caused by evil which was not instantly swung into equipoise by goodness? But these slender reflections troubled him only for a little time. He had little desire for any introspective quarryings. To feel so well was sufficient in itself. Why should thought be so apparent to us, so insistent? Why have we to think aloud and travel laboriously from syllogism to ergo, chary of our conclusions and distrustful of our premises? Thought, as we know it, is a disease and no more. The healthy mentality should register its convictions and not its labours. Our ears should not hear the clamor of its doubts nor be forced to listen to the pro and con wherewith we are eternally badgered and perplexed.

Do remember that this is Stephens's Philosopher, not C. S. Lewis.

3

Spirit

THE ADOLESCENT LEWIS saw irony when there was none, and missed irony when his world was redolent of it. Bondage, indeed: "I did not see what is now the most shining and obvious thing; the Divine humility which will accept a convert on such [grudging] terms." Very likely the conversion was no sudden "plunge into a new life," but rather, as Warren has written, "a slow steady convalescence from a deep-seated spiritual illness of long standing," his neurotic "atheism." Lewis chose to surrender to all the self-sacrificing and unself-regarding ironies of Christian belief. It is startling to learn that when he first became a Christian he did not even believe in an afterlife. With this characteristically willful disregard for himself (again, "willed selflessness"—Christian duty mattering more than Christian destiny), he could seem to those around him to be a curious mix of enthusiastic affection and quite sheer reticence, while all along he was spiritually regressing, a most committed "spiritual alumnus," to use Barfield's image. And as for the charge of wish-fulfillment often leveled against Christians, especially converts to the faith. To paraphrase Lewis, if his purpose were to fulfill wishes, even a dull man could think up something far easier than Christianity; and I would add that Lewis could have contrived a far more convenient life.

Ferociously attentive, selflessly appreciative of what he saw, and relentlessly applicative of what he learned from what he saw, this prodigal son at last returned, but with a difference. The original Prodigal Son at least returned home voluntarily. "But who can duly adore that Love," he wrote, "which will open the high gates to a prodigal who is brought in kicking, struggling, resentful and darting his eyes in every direction for a chance of escape? The words *compelle intrare*, compel them to come in, have been so abused by wicked men that we shudder at them; but, properly understood, they plumb the depth of the Divine mercy. The hardness of God is kinder than the softness of men, and His compulsion is our liberation." To be sure, there was more rinsing yet to be done; but Lewis had made his spiritual and vocational commitment.

I

In a letter written in 1946, Lewis summarized his conversion. He noted that he was baptized in the Church of Ireland and that he and his parents went regularly to church, though they were not particularly pious. His faith was first undermined, he writes, by modern school editions of classical writers: the notes always assumed that pagan religion was utterly false. Why, then, couldn't ours be too? A pair of teachers, including Kirkpatrick, rounded off his disbelief. After a decade and a half of hypocrisy and agnosticism, by which he must mean his various beliefs during the renewed search of his twenties, he was brought back, he says, by four influences: first, philosophy—as of the writing of the letter he continues to maintain that Berkeley is irrefutable; second, medieval literature—How could all those poets and philosophers be wrong?; third, George MacDonald and G. K. Chesterton; and fourth, the Great War, which compelled him to abandon his mechanistic *weltanschauung* forever.

The letter, impressively concise and revealing, is hardly longer than my summary. The four influences effected what Lewis calls Faith-A, initial belief, rather than Faith-B, "obstinacy [Lewis's phrase] in belief" when that initial belief is shaken. As he moved from one to the other his spiritual influences went farther afield than those mentioned above. These are the influences that would cultivate Lewis's Unknown self, as I have called it, and help him in his attempt to "expunge" from it that "pestilent notion of personality." His own conception of spirituality would become characteristic: "Women sometimes have the problem of trying to judge by artificial light how a dress will look by daylight. That is very like the problem of all of us: to dress our souls not for the electric lights of the present world but for the daylight of the next. The good dress is the one that will face that light. For that light will last longer." He would already have encountered Samuel Alexander's argument in *Space, Time and Deity* that religion is in our constitution: "*God is moving us towards achieving deity*; religion is the realization of this movement [emphasis added]." Later he would read St. Ignatius, who describes the goal of spirituality by defining the species (and thus providing some insight into a source of what I will call Lewis's anthropology): "Man was created to praise, reverence and serve our creator and Lord, and by this means to save his soul." His touchstones would be as eclectic, his beliefs as consistent, and his practices as exacting, as one would expect of Lewis.

In January of 1930 he was writing to Arthur of Jacob Boehme that his *Supersensual Dialogue* was easygoing but the *Signatura Rerum* (1621) was not; in fact, he said it was "hopelessly beyond" him, and not merely mystifying. These two sentences from the *Signatura* particularly moved and excited Lewis: "That the nothing is become an eternal life and has found itself, which cannot be, in the Stillness" and "The wrath extinguishes and the turning orb stands still, and instead of the turning a sound is caused in the essence." Is it any wonder that Lewis was alarmed? He told Arthur that it was "the biggest shaking up" since *Phantastes* and that if it continued to give him the same feeling when he understood it more—this one year after becoming a Theist and one before becoming a Christian—he would give it up: "No fooling about for me." But he did keep it up and presently quoted other sentences: "That many a twig withers in the tree is not the tree's fault, for it withdraws its sap from no twig, only the twig gives forth itself too eagerly with the desire: *It runs on in self-will*" (emphasis added) and "He [a penitent] breaks self-hood as a vessel wherein he lies captive, and buds forth continually in God's will-spirit."

Boehme (1575-1624) was a farmer's son and a shoemaker who claimed that his books came "by impulse of the Spirit," as though "dictated." His most famous is *The Way of Christ* (1624), which expresses much religious exaltation, very often quite obscurely, and not a little intolerance. For example, the Roman church was the Wolf, but Lutheranism—"another anti-Christ"—the Fox. But he emphasized a motif that would occupy and preoccupy Lewis his whole life: "Thou must thyself be the way," he prescribed, if "the spiritual understanding must be born in thee." Otherwise a man breaks off from the "Universal will" and by "contraction" withdraws into "self-seeking";

this breaks the "perfect temperature," the "harmonious balance of qualities," and turns the man towards the "dark world." We must "beget" that which is good "out of ourselves. If we make an angel of ourselves we are that; if we make a devil of ourselves we are that." Christ's habitation is the soul's immortal dowry; He is born and lives "in our Nothingness." Thus must we "slay the will." It is understandable that with growing fame and influence would come suppression, for Boehme's prescriptions were radically independent. Lewis would have been hospitable to them, but he was also selective. For example, he would not subscribe to Boehme's Hell, descriptions of which were, claimed Boehme, the results of seeing the real thing.

Among Boehme's followers were the Quakers, Emerson, and, eventually and devotedly, William Law, who came to Boehme some twenty years after the publication (1728) of his *A Serious Call to a Devout and Holy Life* (among Lewis's own most heavily annotated volumes). This book was not only polemical but devotional and mystical, an early indication of his belief in the Inner Light of Quakers. That late development caused some estrangement from his followers, but no one ever questioned his goodness. Lewis must have been impressed by his virtuous adherence to his professed belief (just as he would later admire Sir Walter Scott's literary drudgery to pay off his debts). "Do I beg of God to deal with me, not according to my merit, but according to his own great goodness, and I shall be so absurd as to withhold charity from a poor brother because he may perhaps not deserve it?" So Lewis was not the first who refused to worry—unlike Albert, Warnie, and Tolkien, especially Tolkien, on his behalf—over being "taken in." Law also gave Lewis advice on praying, that it need have no special time or form, and on prayer: "[It] is the nearest approach to God and the highest enjoyment of him. . . . the noblest exercise of the soul, the most excellent use of our best faculties."

In the Advertisement to the first edition of his Analogy (1736), Joseph Butler described both his age and ours, and thus vindicated the work of both Law and of Lewis: "It is come, I know not how, to be taken for granted by many persons that Christianity is not so much as a subject for inquiry, but that it is now at length discovered to be fictitious. . . . as if . . . this were an agreed upon point among all people of discernment and nothing remained but to set it up as a principal subject of mirth and ridicule, as it were by way of reprisals for its having so long interrupted the pleasures of the world." Even after the estrangement Law was unwilling to separate from his church, attending all its services despite the unfriendliness to which he was subjected. Later, John Wesley would say that Law "is hardly to be equalled" and Dr. Johnson—Dr. Johnson!— that Law was "quite an overmatch for me."

We well know of Richard Baxter as the source of Lewis's signature phrase "Mere Christianity." Apparently Baxter used its fullest expression in Church-History of the Government of Bishops (1680) when proclaiming "of what Party" he is: "[I]f you know not," he says, then "I will tell you, I am a CHRISTIAN, a MEER CHRISTIAN, of no other religion." He continues, "I am against all Sects and dividing Parties: But if any will call Meer Christians by the name of a Party, because they take up with meer Christianity, Creed, and Scripture, and will not be of any dividing or contentious Sect, I am of that Party which is so against Parties . . . one that hath no Religion, but that which by Christ and the Apostles was left to the Catholic Church, or the Body of Jesus Christ on Earth." In keeping with his sectlessness, Baxter always recommended moderation, for example advising Dissenters to stay in the Church of England (a good reason, by the way, to believe that Lewis could not have converted to Catholicism, notwithstanding "pious opinions" and practices that he held apart from the trunk of Mere Christianity and thus from his apologetic vocation).

In addition to Baxter three other seventeenth-century divines won Lewis's particular devotion, George Herbert (1593-1633), Jeremy Taylor (1613-67), and, especially, Thomas Traherne. Herbert was an Anglican priest and Orator at Cambridge; considered a saintly man, he was very highly regarded by his contemporaries. He is best known for his poetry, of course, but his *Sketches of a Parson* deserves attention as well. In "The Parson in Mirth," Herbert allows that passion, sin, and misery naturally make for a general sadness but that the parson must "refresh himself as Nature ordains," for "pleasantness of disposition is a great key to do good" and "instructions seasoned with pleasantness both enter sooner and root deeper." Thus the parson ought to "condescend to human frailties both in himself and others, and intermingle some mirth in his discourses occasionally according to the pulse of the hearer." Some of his poems from *The Temple* surely must have been as impressive to Lewis as the prose; for example, "The Forerunners": "The harbingers are come./ See, see their mark;/ White is their color. . . ." Lewis's own "The day with the White Mark," with its talk of omens of joy, is a clear echo.

Jeremy Taylor, who took holy orders and was both married and imprisoned twice, sought the union of all churches on the basis of the Apostle's Creed. In his *Rule and Exercises of Holy Living,* he placed great emphasis on the present, not the future and grand designs, but the business at hand: all "considerations," he said—in direct opposition to Screwtape—must be "reduced to Practice." Taylor, however, did not win Lewis's devotion as did Traherne, whose *Centuries of Meditation* Lewis called "almost the most beautiful book . . . in English"; he would spend thirty years commenting upon, recommending, and just as surely being influenced by it. "You never enjoy the world aright till . . . you are clothed with the heavens and crowned with the stars," Traherne tells us, because "the world is the beautiful frontispiece to Eternity." Souls, he writes "were made to love and are dark and vain and comfortless till they do it. Till they love they are idle or misemployed. Till they love they are desolate. . . ." Is it any wonder that Lewis is among those who love him greatly? The very titles of his *Poems of Felicity* beckon the soul: "Wonder," "Innocence," "News (from a Foreign Country Came)," "On Leaping Over the Moon (I saw new world beneath the water lie, new people)" (not unlike the royal entourage that Lewis describes in *The Voyage of the Dawn Treader*?). But this next poem must have been among those that most dearly spoke to Lewis; it is from "Desire" and explains Traherne's gratitude:

> *For giving me desire,*
> *An eager thirst, a burning ardent fire,*
> *A virgin infant flame,*
> *A love with which into the world I came,*
> *An inward hidden heavenly love,*
> *Which my soul did work and move,*
> *And ever, ever me inflame*
> *With restless longing, heavenly avarice,*
> *That never could be satisfied,*
> *That did incessantly a Paradise*
> *Unknown suggest, and something undescribed*
> *Discern, and bear me to it; be*
> *Thy name forever praised by me.*

Lewis himself never exceeded this description, explanation, and praise of Joy.

But even Traherne was not the "sweetest" of writers. For Lewis, that was St. Francis de Sales, another early seventeenth-century spiritual writer whom he recommended promiscuously. The saint's *Introduction to the Devout Life* (1609) achieved immediate and wide-spread popularity. It is principally a manual but also an apologetic, imagining characters, answering objections, commonly drawing analogies, and sprinkling examples throughout; and it is rich in the psychology of an ordinary believer, most of all with respect to temptation and its antidotes. Lewis valued this familiar quality most, along with its reiterated advice, to first "put yourself in the presence of God." In fact, he valued this book as a balance to Thomas à Kempis's *The Imitation of Christ* (1418), which he visited regularly for meditational and devotional purposes, but "a little bit at a time, more like sucking a lozenge than eating a slice of bread."

He thought *The Imitation* "astringent" and perhaps too severe, and certainly not for reading during times of discouragement. Intended largely for monks, it seemed addressed to "creatures without wings" who every day are "reading about the stratosphere." There are many sections that must have influenced Lewis's spiritual life and that might be sources for his own work; for example, chapter xvi, "The Suffering of Other Men's Faults," bears comparison to "The Trouble with 'x' . . .". But two passages merit quotation because of the light they shed on a certain aspect of Lewis's approach—at once reasoning and reticent—to certain doctrines. Virtually at the beginning of his book, Kempis writes, "What availeth it to reason high secret mysteries of the Trinity if a man lack meekness, whereby he displeaseth the Trinity. Truly nothing. For high curious reasons make not a man holy or rightwise, but a good life maketh him beloved with God. I had rather feel compunc-

tion of heart for my sins than only to know the definition of
compunction." He amplifies upon the theme of intellectual
limits throughout the book and dozens of chapters later addresses a question that Lewis would virtually dismiss in his
Letters to Malcolm, the dynamic of Holy Communion. Kempis
warns that "Thou must be ware of a curious and an unprofit-
able searching of this most profound Sacrament, if thou will
not be drowned in . . . doubt. Blessed is that simplicity that
leaveth the way of hard questions. . . . Go therefore with a pure
and undoubting faith, and with an humble reference proceed
to this Sacrament. . . . in ways unsearchable, high above all reason." Or, as Lewis would put it, "The command, after all, was
Take, eat: not Take, understand."

II

Lewis was variously nourished, instructed, buoyed, and mo-
tivated by many other writers, of course, several of which he
recommends to readers and to correspondents, sometimes with
an interesting piece of advice. If they find that when they kneel
down to pray, or get down to a book of devotions, nothing
happens, then "they might find that the heart sings unbidden
while they are working their way through a tough bit of theology with . . . a pencil in their hand." Thus, in such a combination of reverence and thoughtfulness, might he have
learned that Rudolph Otto is right in saying that the Christian God enables belief because his attributes are meaningful—they add up "to a concept" but are "not comprehended
in them." That is why, adds Otto at the very beginning of *The
Idea of the Holy*, that holiness is an "*a priori* category of the
mind." All of this Lewis, in his unparalleled capacity to ab-
sorb, would have learned, one way or another. Or he could
have learned close to all of it from George MacDonald.

MacDonald lived virtually the whole of the nineteenth-century (1824-1905) and wrote in several genres. Though rejected early on by his congregation, he was much admired by his contemporaries. He supported his large family with his vast output of writing, much of which is coming back into print. Lewis included him as a character in *The Great Divorce*, having him discuss the difficult questions of what constitutes Purgatory and why severe judgment is both necessary and not cruel when applied to the irremediably self-absorbed. In his preface to *George MacDonald: An Anthology*, which he edited, Lewis famously wrote, "In making this collection I was discharging a debt of justice. I have never concealed the fact that I regarded him as my master; indeed I fancy I have never written a book in which I did not quote from him." A bit less famously he wrote in that same preface the sort of thing aptly applied to Lewis himself: "I will attempt no historical or theological classification . . . because I am no friend to such pigeonholing. One very effective way of silencing the voice of conscience is to impound in an *Ism* the teacher through whom it speaks: the trumpet no longer seriously disturbs our rest when we have murmured 'Thomist,' 'Barthian,' or 'Existentialist.' And in MacDonald it is always the voice of conscience that speaks." He adds that he is not producing a critical text, and presumably he is not producing a representative collection of MacDonald's work. But it is not a stretch to assume that Lewis's choices reflect his own preferences, perhaps those which were most useful and nourishing to his own spiritual life.

Of the 365 entries, only six deal with feeling, all six with feeling in its proper place; religious emotion does not rank high. On the other hand, ten entries discuss a philosophy of nature in one way or another, with a resolute insistence on the concrete. Eight deal with fear in one's spiritual life, and they are "as golden and genial as Traherne, but also as astringent

as *The Imitation.*" There are also entries—the titles are
Lewis's—on one's critics, self-control, self-denial, pain and joy,
"When We Do Not Find Him," solitude, death, and the mystery of evil. "A man does not live by his feelings," MacDonald
writes in response to the fear that one is not feeling as one
ought at his devotions, "any more than by bread." That is
number twenty-seven. Number twenty-eight is the first of a
handful on dryness: "And when he can no longer *feel* the truth,
he shall not therefore die. He lives because God is true; and
he is able to know that he lives because he knows, having once
understood the word that God is truth. He believes in the God
of the former vision, lives by that word therefore, when all is
dark and there is no vision." Does it seem as though Lewis
might have had MacDonald opened at his elbow much of the
time? "Our Lord never thought," we read in forty-three, "to
be original." And in 185 Lewis offers what might have been a
slogan of his own: "Human science is but the backward un-
doing of the tapestry-web of God's science, works with its back
to Him, and is always leaving Him—His intent, that is, His
perfected work—behind it, always going farther and farther
away from the point where his work culminates in revelation."
Nature, as Lewis experienced it, for example, on his many
walking tours, is not a theory but a perpetual delight to the
senses and a message, analyzable by science but not therefore
explained by it.

Along with entries on fear and dryness, I believe these on
the self and its aspects are the most telling. In "The Eternal
Round" we read, "Obedience is the joining of the links of the
eternal round. Obedience is but the other side of the eternal
will. [Lewis said he was not born to be happy, he "was born
to obey."] Will is God's will, obedience is man's will; the two
make one. . . . If we do the will of God, eternal life is ours"—

close to a platitude, but MacDonald adds exactly what Lewis does in telling us that we can become sons, instead of creatures, of God—"no mere continuity of existence, for that in itself is worthless as hell, but a being that is one with the essential life." While writing his autobiography and telling the reader about being brought in "kicking and screaming," Lewis might have had in mind "A Man's Right": "[T]o be compelled to repent; to be hedged in on every side: to have one after another of the strong, sharp-toothed sheep dogs of the Great Shepherd sent after him, to thwart him in any desire, foil him in any plan, frustrate him of any hope, until he come to see at length that nothing will ease his pain, nothing make life a thing worth having, but the presence of the living God within him."

I have suggested that the self can be likened to a window, an opening through which a wind, or a "spirit," might pass. Part of Lewis's self remained sealed, a portion of it by him, another *from* him (as the Johari window predicts). It seems clear that he is giving the reasoning self dangerously too much credit in this mix, ignoring first his mother's, then his father's death, then the great deal of pain he had suffered (some self-inflicted), and finally the whole landscape of the Unknown Self that kept the Inner life, as Lewis has called it, vital. The book Lewis should have written but did not was a systematic study on the self: should have, because at bottom he discussed little else in much of his work and his own self is so prominent in that work; did not, because he failed to quite understand his own self but knew that he must escape it. The notion of "personality" that he would expunge is merely a projection of the self. His poem "Legion," originally published in 1955, not only addresses this point but applies it:

Lord, hear my voice, my present voice, I mean,
Not that which may be speaking an hour hence
(For I am Legion) in an opposite sense,
And not by show of hands decide between
The multiple factions which my state has seen
Or will see. Condescend to the pretense
That what speaks now is I; in its defence
Dissolve my parliament and intervene.

Thou wilt not, though we asked it, quite recall
Free will once given. Yet to this moment's choice
Give unfair weight. Hold me to this. Oh strain
A point—use legal fictions; for if all
My quarrelling selves must bear an equal voice
Farewell, thou hast created me in vain.

In a place as unlikely as his massive Oxford literary history volume, Lewis exalts over a similar achievement. After describing what it must have felt like to be an early Protestant, he shows that a life of "voluntary gloom" was "exactly what the first Protestants would have forbidden," for grace abounding would have made them joyful—grace, not their own paltry works. "From this buoyant humility, this farewell to the self with all its good resolutions, anxiety, scruples, and motive-scratchings, all the Protestant doctrines originally sprang."

MacDonald's final two statements on the self in Lewis's anthology (which I conflate) not only affirm this spiritual vector in Lewis but provide the basis for his only formal, explicit, and brief discussion which departs markedly from the master, an essay entitled "Two Ways with the Self." Here is MacDonald:

I sickened at the sight of Myself; how should I ever get rid of the demon? The same instant I saw the one escape: I must offer it back to its source—commit it to Him who made it. I must live no more from it but from the source of it. . . . What flashes of self-consciousness might cross me, should be God's gift, not of my seeking . . . and offered again to Him. . . . [But] vain were the fancy, by treatise, or sermon, or poem, or tale, to persuade a man to forget himself. He cannot if he would. Sooner will he forget the presence of a raging tooth. There is no forgetting of ourselves but in the finding of our deeper, our true self—God's idea of us when He devised us— the Christ in us. Nothing but that self can displace the false, greedy, whining self, of which most of us are so fond and proud.

Of the aging master, Hannah Tatum Pearsall Smith (mother of Logan Pearsall Smith) wrote in a letter to friends in 1893 that "We have had another most honored guest . . . and that is George MacDonald. . . . He is the dearest old man, so gentle and yet so strong, and with such a marvellous insight into spiritual things. He is like an old patriarch who embraces the whole world as his family, and spreads hands of blessing over all."

Lewis opens "Two Ways with the Self" (originally published in the *Guardian* on May 3, 1940) by noting an apparent contradiction. St. Francis de Sales, Lady Julian of Norwich, and the New Testament bid us not to resent ourselves, to be mild in our self-remonstrances and loving and peaceful towards ourselves, and to love ourselves; on the other hand, Jesus says that a true disciple must hate his own life. The difference, Lewis adds, is not one of degree. Rather, it is in the two ways in which the self can be regarded: as God's creature, now in a hateful condition and thus to be pitied and healed, but nevertheless an occasion of joy; or as the only self called "I" or "me," it has an irrational claim to preference. It is the latter which is to be killed. Quoting MacDonald, Lewis writes that it must never "be allowed a moment's respite from eternal death." However, although the Christian is relentless in his battle against the ego as such, he loves *selves*. When he has learned to love his neighbor as himself—"which will hardly be in this life," Lewis adds—he might then "love himself as his neighbor: that is, with charity instead of partiality." Then Lewis closes with a frightening, powerfully clarifying passage that would be the basis for many future characters, episodes, and expository passages, and not without some muted irony:

> The other kind of self-hatred, on the contrary, hates selves as such. It begins by accepting the special value of the particular self called *me*; then, wounded in its pride to find that such a darling object should be so disappointing, it seeks revenge, first upon that self, then on all. Deeply egoistic, but now with an inverted egoism, it uses the revealing argument, "I don't spare myself"—with the implication "then *a fortiori* I need not spare others".... The wrong asceticism torments the self: the right kind kills the selfness. We must die daily: but it is better to love the self than to love nothing, and to pity the self than to pity no one.

Thus "sickened at the sight of Myself" and "demon" are images that Lewis, unlike MacDonald, would not apply to himself, or to any self, as opposed to its sins.

Still, we are not told what a self is. Maybe my figure of an open window wants re-figuring, its implication of perfect freedom, and thus of perfect clarity, being false. "Spirit" certainly meant wind, but for a Christian it can mean light, and light may pass through a lens onto the receiving spirit, though not, depending on the lens, without some distortion and loss. The problem arises when we pay improper attention to the lens, forgetting that the best one is the plainest, the "poorest" in adornment and complication, and thus the clearest. When we are not only known by God but assent to being known, "then," Lewis writes in *Letters to Malcolm*, "we treat ourselves, in relation to God, not as things but as persons. We have unveiled." MacDonald sums up beautifully. This is from his book of devotional poetry, *Diary of an Old Soul*, the poem for November 7:

> *Wilt thou not one day, Lord? In all my wrong,*
> *self-love and weakness, laziness and fear,*
> *This one thing I can say: I am content*
> *To be and have what in thy heart I am meant*
> *To be and have. In my best times I long*
> *After thy will, and think it glorious-dear;*
> *Even in my worst, perforce my will to thine is bent.*

III

In the letter summarized at the beginning of this chapter, Lewis mentions the influence of the medieval worldview in the context of his conversion for the first and (I believe) the last time. Of course, he does specify the poets and philosophers, "worldview" being my word; but writers and thinkers could not be separated from the image that he would so ably describe in his famous introductory lectures and the book based upon them, *The Discarded Image*. It was a Catholic world, full of correspondences between nature and supernature, sacramentalism, authority and hierarchy, demands for obedience, selflessness (artists and builders, for example, would routinely not sign their work), debate among the learned, and a "pas-

sionate intensity of life," to use the words of the great medi-
evalist Johan Huizinga, who opens his seminal *The Autumn
of the Middle Ages* with the observation that "The distance between sadness and joy, between good and bad fortune, seemed
to be much greater than for us; every experience had that
degree of directness and absoluteness that Joy and sadness still
have in the mind of a child. Every event, every deed was
defined in given and expressive forms and was in accord with
the solemnity of a tight, invariable life style. The great events
of human life—birth, marriage, death—by virtue of the sacraments, basked in the radiance of the divine mystery."

Although not perfectly, this medieval landscape comfortably accommodates a dimension of Lewis, and his affinity to
the period bespeaks a deep stratum and strong intensity of
spiritual responsiveness that complements without subvert-
ing the intellectualized view he took of his own conversion.
But few people in the Middle Ages could have been as intellectually eclectic as Lewis, as free to read, think, and choose
as they pleased; and the world would soon be Protestant. So
I would not press the point—an affinity for the Middle Ages
that goes beyond the literary—any further. It should not escape us, though, that he says nothing of medievalism in *Surprised by Joy* and nothing of Joy in the letter; nor does he ever
note the fit of the latter to the former. And he never sees the
intellectual resemblances—yes, amidst very great differences—
between Anthroposophy and the medieval world-picture.

Lewis excludes from his intellectual inventory anything
that smacks even remotely of an *existential* explanation of the
self—an approach to being and choosing, to defining the self
by Enjoyment, to use Alexander's terms, rather than by Contemplation—for which he had no sympathy whatever and
towards whose avatars he expressed puzzlement, mild amuse-

ment, and disbelief. The disregard was unfortunate, eventually disadvantageous in serious ways. But he certainly intu-
ited both its utility and its ontological reality. While discussing
Chesterton in *Surprised by Joy*, for example, he sought to understand the writer's "immediate conquest" when in fact there
should have been antipathy: "It would almost seem that Provi-
dence, or some 'second cause' of a very obscure kind, quite
over-rules our previous tastes when It decides to bring two
minds together. Liking an author may be as involuntary and
improbable as falling in love," or as converting. Lewis would
be surprised by both. My hypothesis is the existence of Lewis's
Deeper life, the spiritual world that was being and choosing
and defining on behalf of Lewis's Outer and Inner lives all
along. The spiritual genius often works without the help or
knowledge of its colleagues.

Axiomatically, then, no one's spirituality is evident, least
of all in the case of someone who is reticent about it, reticent
even with himself. At least initially, therefore, Lewis's is best
approached—as he made his approach both in life and in literature—obliquely. What did he do? For example, of the
fourteen Works of Mercy, seven Spiritual and seven Corporal, which did he undertake? The seven Corporal Works of
Mercy, based upon Christ's prediction of the Last Judgment
in the Gospel of St. Matthew 5:3-10, are these: feed the hungry, give drink to the thirsty, clothe the naked, shelter the
homeless, visit the sick, visit those in prison, and bury the dead.
We know that Lewis performed six of these.

On occasion he would tend to some stranger who came
begging or whom he encountered, sometimes to the conster-
nation of those around him. Often he gave away money anonymously and, to avoid credit for the act, under some pretense,
claiming to needy students, for example, that a special schol-

arship fund existed precisely for the particular need of that student. He sheltered blitz evacuees in his home. And he established a trust fund, in existence to this day and for a long while in receipt of two-thirds of his growing income, the moneys from which were distributed variously, anonymously of course, and in many cases continuously to the same needy people. He was commonly viewed as a "soft touch," and his closest friends, as we have noted, simply thought he could be "taken in."

His performance of these mercies was habitual, and he responded to objections as MacDonald would have, and as Calvin may have taught them both to do, with the assertion that it is better to be taken in than not to undertake an act of genuine mercy. In his Oxford literary history Lewis allows that "few men have written better than Calvin" on this matter and then quotes him: "[F]or Scripture here cometh to our aide with this excellent reason, that we respect not what men merit of themselves but looke only upon God's image which they bear."

We know that he visited, and cared for, the sick and helped to bury the dead; we do not know, however, that he did these acts for strangers or that he visited those in prison (just as we do not know that he did not). Here we should take note of his care for Mrs. Moore. It is with her that his suppressed emotions had "avenged" themselves and who was, first insufferable, next towards the end of her life gravely and chronically ill, then insane, and finally all at once. Lewis never relented in the care he both provided for her and showed her personally—a lifelong habit. The indenture early had become an unhappy one, having assumed the status of raw duty. At the end it surely had become a penance.

The seven Spiritual Works of Mercy are converting sinners, instructing the ignorant, counseling the doubtful, comforting the sorrowful, bearing wrongs patiently, forgiving injuries, and praying for the living and the dead. Lewis's discharge of most of these is obvious, indeed so obvious that the magnitude of his devotion is often taken lightly. The first two consumed most of his adult life, and at no inconsiderable expense. Some academics complained that he should have been more professionally productive than he was, done more scholarship, written more books. Perhaps he agreed, and we know he would have been, had he not committed himself to a vocation. We cannot know for sure that he would have preferred writing scholarly books to apologetic ones, and he must have enjoyed the writing of the latter since they allowed such scope to his "expository demon" and the argumentative man. But he did not enjoy answering the many thousands of letters that he received, nor waking up at four o'clock in the morning, which he did for a long stretch during the war, to answer them. He did not enjoy giving those lectures at Royal Air Force bases: not only did he think them a failure at first, but the mere coming and going were burdensome. And he did not enjoy the jealousy that his fame engendered and which probably, though not solely, cost him a professorship at Oxford. In short, his public ministry and its epistolary offshoot were a costly burden, but not so costly that he ever thought to stop.

He counseled and comforted without surcease, perhaps more by letter than in person; but there is testimony to the effectiveness of his personal counseling, especially from former students. He was neither of a time, temperament, place, nor generation that invited "sharing," but when the need to comfort came his way and he thought it legitimate to do so, he apparently was quite good at it. Yet he was probably better at bearing wrongs patiently and forgiving injuries. He is not known to have complained about suffering wrongs or to have carried a grudge; on the other hand, he seems to have avoided occasions that would give rise to either. His marriage, for example, caused no little confusion; and Joy Davidman—a difficult woman—courted ill will. When antagonism arose, however, Lewis simply withdrew from those who might show it. Some friendships cooled, others effectively ended. Lewis probably thought that those people were the ones doing the choosing, opting against the new terms of friendship which necessarily included, not only Joy and all her works, but a different Jack, too; and he would not think to patronize them as though they had chosen badly.

Five of the seven Spiritual Works of Mercy play to Lewis's great genius, the presiding *daemon*, the voluble self. They require speech or its surrogates. So it is reasonable that, of the seven, the one that most occupied Lewis—that aroused both his spiritual and intellectual geniuses—was prayer. Not only does he seem curious about it, but he must have found the subject most on the minds of people who queried him: how, what, where, and when to pray, and the workings of prayer, along with its paradoxes, such as just who is speaking to whom when one prays. He wrote "The Efficacy of Prayer," "Petitionary Prayer: A Problem Without an Answer," several poems, very many letters on prayer, and of course *Letters to Malcolm: Chiefly on Prayer*, a largely devotional, rather than expository, book and the culmination, really, of his spiritual thinking. The late Dom Bede Griffiths—a spiritual writer and guide, a mystic of considerable note, and once Lewis's pupil, converting, though to Catholicism, at the same time as Lewis—said of his former tutor that he possessed "a profound kind of mystical intuition" and in *Malcolm* "comes near to a genuine mystical insight." "We have no non-religious" activities, Lewis wrote in this extraordinary book, and the particular activity of prayer is the most intimate we will ever know.

If at this point there arises the old and troublesome question of Faith versus Works as our primary route to salvation, then let me side with Lewis, who says the following in his Oxford literary history: "The theological questions really at issue have no significance except on a certain . . . high level of the spiritual life; they could have been fruitfully debated only between mature and saintly disputants in close privacy and at boundless leisure." He would maintain this and many another rhetorical caveat, especially about questions so rootedly controversial and which he thought less important than many others to the definition and defense of Mere Christianity.

As for himself, he prayed almost anywhere and at any time; sometimes verbally but other times not; he often said a set prayer, but even then "festooned" it, as he tells us in *Malcolm*. When he was able to kneel he did so; and he prayed for both the living and the dead. His most notable instance of prayer was the set he said over his dying, pain-stricken, cancer-ridden wife. As Father Peter Bide, a friend, former pupil, and Anglican priest with a reputation for having a healing touch, laid hands on both Jack and Joy, Lewis prayed that his wife would live and, even if she did not, that her suffering be taken from her and passed on to him. Her pain was relieved, he not only felt great pain but developed incipient osteoporosis, and Joy's pelvic cancer was healed—that is, her pelvis grew back. "This is why prayer must come before everything else," writes John Paul II in his address to the young at New Orleans (March 14, 1979). "People who do not take this view," he continues, "who do not put this into practice, cannot plead the excuse of being short of time; what they are short of is love."

When Joy was ill, Lewis began developing a preference for taking Holy Communion privately, but he regarded the practice as unhealthy and discontinued it. He did take Holy Communion at least once a week and certainly believed in the Real Presence, though not in any one theory, such as transubstantiation, purporting to explain it. But he would not reject it. ("Our Lord said Take, eat; not Take, understand.") He would not have shared the invective on this subject of *The Book of Common Prayer*. After the war, Lewis regularly visited a spiritual advisor, Walter Adams of the Cowley Fathers. He confessed his sins orally and on his knees. He believed in Purgatory because he believed in the need for purgation: if we are to appear before a great King, it is only proper to prefer that we appear at our spruced up best, he thought. He did make clear, however, that the Purgatory in which he believed was Dante's, not the "degradation" of a temporary Hell as in "Thomas More's *Supplication of Souls*." (I believe Lewis never referred to More as "Saint," a rare exception in his use of that honorific.)

For most of us, beliefs and practices, spiritual or otherwise, evolve, finally becoming organic, vital, and throbbing parts of our internal life. So it was for Lewis. By the mid-1950s, he was a seasoned spiritual veteran, relentlessly self-examining and ruthless with egoism. This led to a remarkable discipline, allowing him to keep his goal always in view. He was adroit: What is needed *now*? And he was realistic: Take *The Imitation* in small doses, and follow it with Traherne or de Sales. Stay concrete, not worrying or wondering about abstractions. Be severe with the self without being punitive. But very far above all obey, which he said he was born to do. ("We have no 'Right to Happiness,'" as he would entitle one of his most severe essays.) He sometimes may have fallen short, but his standards were uncompromising, and changing them was simply out of the question. In his own spiritual development he was—and would have us be in ours—utterly unsentimental.

As with his literary life, so with his spiritual, the former closely following the latter in its stages. The exposition and defense of ideas had had its place as allegory, parable, romance, and debate. By the time he wrote *The Problem of Pain* (1940) he had come to terms intellectually with the problem of will, saying "A man can no more diminish God's glory by refusing to worship Him than a lunatic can put out the sun by scribbling the word 'darkness' on the walls of his cell. But God wills our good, and our good is to love him." By the 1950s he would write in *Reflections on the Psalms* (1958), that "there is almost no 'letter' in the words of Jesus. . . . No net less wide than a man's whole heart, nor less fine of mesh than love, will hold the sacred fish." And perhaps the pope was influenced by this observation, which has little at all to do with will, from *The Four Loves* (1960, though recorded as radio talks in late summer of 1958 for broadcast in the United States): "a man's spiritual health is exactly proportional to his love for"—not his obedience to—"God." And in his book on the Psalms he ponders the old question of what we were made for and where, but turns the answer from one of exposited theology to a figure of speech. He notes the sacramental strangeness of the world and writes, in a tone that combines both Chesterton and MacDonald, "It is as strange as if a fish were repeatedly surprised at the wetness of water. And that would be strange indeed, unless of course the fish were destined to become, one day, a land animal."

William Nicholson, author of the stage and film version of *Shadowlands*, quite astonished me when he said that he had chosen Lewis for a romantic treatment because, like Nicholson himself, Lewis "came late to commitment," which he could learn only through pain and which, until he met Joy and suffered with her, he had known only abstractly, not actually. Flora's death, and Albert's; the blood, death, and destruction of the trenches of World War I; Warnie's alcoholism; the loss of Charles Williams; the lifelong care-giving to Mrs. Moore—these and other elements of Lewis's life were apparently un-

impressive to Mr. Nicholson. But they made their mark on
Lewis. After the recovery of faith, the lesson to be learned was
interpretive: along with his unrelenting honesty, and all the
thinking, reading, and attentiveness to nature and to people,
came his interpretive genius. In discussing the levels of meaning in the Psalms, Lewis perfectly breaks down the epistemological point with his characteristic analogic deftness: "For
what is required on all these levels alike, is not merely knowledge but a certain insight; getting the focus right. . . . One who
contended that a poem was nothing but black marks on a paper
would be unanswerable if he addressed an audience who
couldn't read. Look at it through microscopes, analyze the
printer's ink . . . you will never discover something over and
above. . . . Those who can read, however, will continue to say
the poem exists."

Some who knew him saw a certain mystery about him, not
secretiveness or a mere preference for privacy, but actual
mystery. But I say—about a man with so strong a potential
light of his own, so fierce a will to bring it into brightness, and
so clear and clearly focused a self, a lens, as his had become—
how not a Mystery? James Stephens might have spoken for
Lewis when, near the end of *The Crock of Gold*, the
Philosopher's wife realizes that "she was not an individual only;
she was also part of a mighty organism ordained. . . . The duty
of life is the sacrifice of self: it is to renounce the little ego that
the mighty ego may be freed . . . for everything must come
from the Liberty into Bondage, that it may return again to the
Liberty comprehending all things and fitted for that fiery enjoyment . . . [the] keen stir in the air that stung the blood to
joy." As for himself, he made clear that even the weakest language was too strong to communicate the weakness of his own
spirituality.

PART II

BRANCHES

4

Word

THE CENTRAL MODE OF EXPRESSION of any self is speech, the physical manifestation of our participation in the Logos—our share of the Word. Appreciation of speech permeates the whole of Lewis's life, work, and internal landscape. All the societies and clubs; the broadcasts, talks, and sermons; the tutoring and the lectures; the ceaseless conversation and letters, nothing more than a surrogate for speech; all the recitations aloud of favorite passages, the reading aloud of works in progress; the utter, wholly unlikely mastery of the art of oral communication, in any setting, over any medium, to any of several ends, with the utmost discretion and nuance, and with the greatest effect; his prayer—all of these evidence relentlessly Lewis's apprehension of this central fact: The most concrete, palpable, frequent, and important act of human *being* is direct oral communication—same time, same place, face-to-face.

His influence on his contemporaries "was at least as much as orator as writer," wrote Fr. Gervase Mathew, a friend and colleague who for nine years coordinated his lectures with

Lewis's. He took a vivid and sporting interest in the size of his audience, noted Fr. Mathew, and "always forged a personal link with those who heard him." Students regularly stood in auditoriums filled to capacity—a rarity at Cambridge or Oxford—in order to hear his lectures.

But not only did Lewis indulge in speech always and everywhere, he revealed it as fundamental to our human nature, our *redeemable* nature. "Talking too much is one of my vices, by the way," he wrote to a correspondent in 1956. But they are the Talking Beasts of Narnia who know Aslan; it is the uttering of nonsense that effects the demise of the N.I.C.E. in *That Hideous Strength*; it is the hearing of a voice that alters the destiny of John the Pilgrim in *The Pilgrim's Regress*; and Ransom is a philologist whose training and skill enable him to speak with—and thus to dwell among and befriend—the creatures of Malacandra in *Out of the Silent Planet*, creatures who thereafter no longer seem as strange as their mere appearance at first suggested. Of course, as our most frequent and telling instrument of performance, speech is fraught with risk— of inherent distortion and deliberate corruption, of manipulation and betrayal, and of subtle self-deception. Lewis knew all of this, in all his geniuses, but he did not know it all at once.

I

The presiding aspect of the genius of words was the "Old Western Man," as Lewis called himself upon accepting the professorial chair at Cambridge created especially for him, a person who could read old texts as a native and see new ones from the vantage of a long perspective. In his famous inaugural lecture at Cambridge (1954) Lewis discussed divides—fissures, along the edges of which he had dwelled for more than half his life—and dismissed all the "great divides" of Western Civilization (e.g., between the Ancient World and the Dark Ages, the Middle Ages and the Renaissance, the Renaissance and the Enlightenment) as relatively minor when compared with the Great Divide, "that which divides the present from, say the age of Jane Austen and Scott." Our age of machines, political "leaders" (instead of "rulers"), religious skepticism and atheism, and Dadaists, Surrealists, and Picasso is more foreign to old Western culture than any other period within it. Yet this great change, Lewis went on to say, is not even now complete, and "those who are native to different sides of it can still meet. I myself," Lewis stated, "belong far more to that Old Western order than to this one." And he recognized the limits of his affinities, for "you don't want to be lectured on Neanderthal Man by a Neanderthaler, still less on dinosaurs by a dinosaur." Then, in a peroration which since has become very famous, Lewis described why those affinities eminently qualified him for his new position as Professor of Medieval and Renaissance English Literature:

> And yet, is that the whole story? If a live dinosaur dragged its slow length into the laboratory, would we not all look back as we fled? What a chance to know at last how it really moved and looked and smelled and what noises it made! . . . One thing I know: I would give a great deal to hear any ancient Athenian, even a stupid one, talking about Greek tragedy. He would know in his bones so much that we seek in vain. . . . Ladies and gentlemen, I stand before you somewhat as that Athenian might stand. I read as a native texts which you must read as foreigners. . . . And because this is the judgement of a native, I claim that, even if the defence of my conviction is weak, the fact of my conviction is historical datum to which you should give full weight. That way, where I fail as a critic, I may yet be useful as a specimen.

Note that with characteristic prescience he has described the postmodern world. Of course, he was always a specimen which, as we have already seen, was a function of how he regarded his self—as raw material, a *datum*—and, as we shall see further on, was a great source of his appeal.

His learning and critical skills were so prodigious that, in this case I think, facility must be conceded. Consider this mere inventory: He introduced the "personal heresy" into our critical lexicon, arguing that we are wrong to read a book in order to find out about its author or to study an author's life in order to appreciate his book as a literary artifact, for to do either is to abort the strictly literary experience we are after in the first place. (Here all at once are Albert's rhetorical temper shining forth, Barfield's perception of self-contrivance—*pastiche*, as he called it—and that coyness about a self that he would try to dissuade us from examining, tipped off by Lewis's vastly over-argued protestations.) He described the medieval foundations of romantic love and charted its literary genealogy, breathing life into a calcified notion of allegory—and into many a moribund work—along the way. He defined *Paradise Lost* for a generation, debunking the Satan-as-hero error as he did so: "From hero to general, from general to politician, from politician to secret service agent, then to a thing that peers in at bedroom or bathroom windows, and thence to a toad, and finally to a snake." He revised our understanding of English literature in the sixteenth century, plausibly arguing that there was no Renaissance in England and that, if there was, it did not matter. He unfolded to us the medieval worldview so that we can never again think of those ancestors as particularly ignorant, superstitious, or irrational. He described precisely those dozen or so concepts which so ensnare us when we take them for granted. He taught us what

we do, should do, and must not do when we read. He "reha-
bilitated" dozens of authors and shot out of the air as many
literary fallacies as there are critical schools. He also got more
unlikely people to read more old books than ever before by
the sheer force of his enthusiasm. And all of this work is re-
splendently, improbably readable.

The polemical genius, too, worked as unrelentingly as, but
even more single-mindedly than, the scholar to make a great
variety of ideas comprehensible to the general reader. A small
sampling merely of titles suggests that and more, an uncanny
timeliness: "The Humanitarian Theory of Punishment," "Dangers of National Repentance," "The Poison of Subjectivism,"
"The Necessity of Chivalry," "Democratic Education," and "Sex
in Literature."

But, like the great lion Aslan, Lewis was not tame. There
are in his work unlikely opinions that surprise even his most
devoted readers: that young lovers should live together without marriage if the alternative is to break their marriage vows;
that anti-abortion laws may be very ill-advised; that obscen-
ity laws are useless at best, as are anti-sodomy laws; that a truly
Christian economic order would have more than a small bit
of socialism in it; that Darwin is useful even if he mistook a
metaphor that was already in the air (Keats used a version of
evolution in *Hyperion*); and that Freud has something to teach
us, though a good deal less than he thought. No one has ut-
tered a more astute, trenchant, or profoundly Christian critique of the impact of European civilization upon the New
World than Lewis: "The English conceived [colonization]
chiefly as a social sewage system, a vent for 'needy people who
now trouble the commonwealth and are daily consumed with
the gallows'. . . . Nor was the failure [of English exploration]
relieved by any high ideal motives. Missionary designs are

sometimes paraded in the prospectus of a new venture: but the actual record of early Protestantism in this field seems to be 'blank as death'." In "Religion and Rocketry" he expands upon the theme, claiming that "the missionary's holy desire to save souls has not always been kept quite distinct from the arrogant desire, the busybody's itch to (as he calls it) 'civilize' the (as he calls them) 'natives'." And in "The Seeing Eye" he contemplates the possibility of humanity meeting an alien rational species: "I observe how the white man has hitherto treated the black, and how, even among civilized men, the stronger have treated the weaker. . . . I do not doubt that the same story will be repeated. We shall enslave, deceive, exploit, or exterminate."

His general reputation rests largely on his work as an indefatigable dialectician (those obstetrics to which Barfield referred) and as a lifelong poet, in the old Greek sense of "maker." There is no surprise here, given his ineluctable ratiocinative powers and an incandescent imagination. But the scholar (by profession), the poet (by preference and compulsion), and the philosopher (by training) had no grand theories and did not follow schools or invent intricate methodologies. He never wrote what is formally known as systematic theology; remember, he claimed to be no theologian at all, and as we have seen he explicitly shuddered at the notion that his thought might be construed as original. After all, he was an Old, not a New, Western Man. Even as something of an iconoclast Lewis was unassuming, for he would not undertake trendy posturing, employing public angst, for example (our personal proof *du jour*), only near the end of his life in *A Grief Observed*, an idea he elaborated upon as a diary he kept following the death of his wife, and even then as an apologetic effort and under a pseudonym.

These singular achievements become all the more striking as we review the number and variety of his critical works.
Nevill Coghill, a friend and colleague, has lamented the "loss
of his living force in the kind of study in which [he was] engaged, the study of English, of which he was easily the greatest teacher of our time in his chosen fields." And Jeffrey Hart
at once summarized and justified Lewis's influence when he
observed that "To most university students and their profes-
sors, C. S. Lewis is well known as a scholar and a literary critic.
His two books on medieval literature, his books on Milton and
on sixteenth-century literature and his widely ranging essays,
have firmly established his authority in the Academy."

The Allegory of Love: A Study in Medieval Tradition, Lewis's
first major critical work, won for him the Gollancz Memorial
Prize and was described by William Empson as "learned, witty,
and sensible": "In the first flush of renewed admiration for the
Romance of the Rose I tried to read the Chaucerian version
. . . . Far better to read Mr. Lewis." A critic for the *London Times*
wrote that it was a "scholarly, fascinating and original book
. . . . Mr. Lewis is both interested and skilled in the history of
human psychology. He is obviously qualified to write literary history of the best kind; for his book is an example of it."
In *A Preface to Paradise Lost*, Lewis praises Milton for perfectly
imitating, and allowing us to participate in, the great dance
of all Christendom, an achievement owing, for the most part,
to a decorous and harmonious style. *The Personal Heresy*, coyness aside, shows that the function of poetry is *psychagogia*,
enlargement of the mind. In such essays as "The Anthropological Approach" and "Psychoanalysis and Literary Criticism"
he attacks that mode of thought which would violate meaning by taking us out of the structure of the poem and leaving
us there, among the ruins of literary excavations.

The Personal Heresy, ostensibly a debate about Milton's *Paradise Lost* that Lewis conducted with the great literary historian and critic E. M. W. Tillyard, is Lewis's most sustained, albeit oblique, consideration of the self as such. By all accounts, including Tillyard's own, Lewis won by a knockout. A reviewer recorded that "Dr. Tillyard's three studies appear slight when they are confronted with what he rightly calls 'the formidable battery of Mr. Lewis's dialectic,' and his general position seems scarcely tenable. . . . Driven from position to position, Dr. Tillyard returns, wildly, to his original view; but it is a view that has been . . . thoroughly discredited." The theory he forged here seems complete, consistent—and closed.

Lewis's starting point is an attack upon "poetolatry", the practice of reading poetry for the purpose of learning about the poet: "At best we 'shared' or 'looked through' his personality at something else. But . . . it was not, in fact, the personality of a person. More explicitly, it was not a personality at all. It was a mood, or a mode of consciousness, created temporarily in the minds of various readers by the suggestive qualities which certain words and ideas have taken on in the course of human history." Further on, while discussing "the paradox of art, whereby the artist never expresses himself so clearly as when he has suppressed his personality," he states his position more aggressively: "There is something to make the blood run cold in the very idea of offering to a man, even to a dead man like Keats, that same 'willing suspension of disbelief.' . . . The poet is my fellow creature—a traveller between birth and death—one of *us*. . . . I do not owe the poet some aesthetic response: I owe him love, thanks, assistance, justice, charity—or, it may be, a sound thrashing."

When describing the causes of the personal heresy, Lewis remarks upon the nature of reality and, because the dilemma he poses offers only one viable alternative, proceeds to choose sides:

> Surely the dilemma is plain. Either there is significance in the whole process of things as well as in human activity, or there is no significance in human activity itself. It is an idle dream . . . that we can withdraw the human soul, as a mere epiphenomenon, from a universe of idiotic force, and yet hope, after that, to find for her some *faubourg* where she can keep a mock court in exile. . . . If the world is meaningless, then so are we; if we mean something, we do not mean alone. Embrace either alternative, and you are free of the personal heresy.

And free, Lewis might just as well have added, to travel the road right out of the same imperial self necessary, not only to capable criticism and disinterested reading, but to spiritual well-being too.

How "poetry" is such a road depends on one's conception of it. Lewis tells us that poetry is "a skill or trained habit of using all the extra-logical elements of language—rhythm, vowel music, onomatopoeia, associations, and what not to convey the concrete reality of experience," and though only science can tell you when and where you are likely to meet an elm, "only poetry can tell you what meeting an elm is like." Lewis hints at the way poetry acts upon the reader in his analysis of Milton's style in *Paradise Lost*: "He makes his epic a rite so that we may share it; the more ritual it becomes, the more we are elevated to the rank of participants . . . we are summoned . . . to take part . . . in a great mimetic dance of all Christendom, ourselves soaring and running from heaven, ourselves enacting Hell and Paradise, the Fall and the repentance." He notes in *The Personal Heresy* that "there is noth-

ing 'moral' in the narrower sense about this, though morals
come into it." In *An Experiment in Criticism* he adds, "I should
hope to be led . . . to newer and fresher enjoyments, *things I
could never have met [on] my own* [emphasis added]"—if only
we can put aside the self in willing submission to the work.

Two additional literary postulates from *An Experiment in
Criticism* confirm Lewis's view of the absolute necessity for a
disinterested self. The first has to do with the manner in which
literature acts on the reader: "The exercise of our faculties is
in itself a pleasure. Successful obedience to what seems worth
obeying and is not quite easily obeyed is a pleasure. And if
the . . . exercises or the dance is devised by a master, the rest
and movements, the quickenings and slowing, the easier and
more arduous passages, will come exactly as we need them
. . . . looking back on the whole performance, we shall feel that
we have been led through a pattern or arrangement of activities
which our nature cried out for." The second is as ironic as
the first—all along Lewis is insisting that argument has no place
in a literary experience—and affirms both his Protestant independence and his faith in the accessibility of meaning to a
layman: "Whether we regard it as fortunate or unfortunate,
the fact is that there is no essential qualification for criticism
more definite than general wisdom and health of mind."

One of his works that is more well-known than well-read
is *The Abolition of Man*, "Reflections on Education with Special Reference to the Teaching of English in the Upper Forms
of Schools," or so its subtitle would have us think. In fact it
is a diagnosis and a prophesy: When subjectivism is rampantly
triumphant—the imperial self gone crazy—and natural law
has been, not refuted, but "seen through," we begin to "inno-
vate," first on nature (Lewis was environmentally alert long
before the cant began), then on animals (and a vehement anti-

vivisectionist), and finally on our favorite subject, the self, which we will "condition" unto extinction. Any eugenicist or "harvester" of human fetal tissue should take note, if not of this book then of its horrifying fictional correlative, *That Hideous Strength* ("A Modern Fairy Tale for Grown-Ups" and the last book of the Space trilogy, following *Out of the Silent Planet* and *Perelandra*). In it Lewis both raises to glorious heights and lowers to terrifying depths the idea of geniuses as tutelary spirits: the angelic will reject, and the demonic feast upon, *all* the imperial selves, just as David Lindsay described.

Twenty-five years ago members of the New York C. S. Lewis Society responded to a question about Lewis's most appealing feature with such words as *brilliance, clarity, reason, veracity, Britishness, nobility, caritas, humility,* and *joy.* One member praised Lewis as a "lovable, warm person, not a phony"; another, as a man of great patience; and yet a third, as a "sophisticate." And apparently each was correct, for those who had met Lewis personally and addressed the Society all remarked upon these very same qualities. As Thomas Howard put it, he was "down to the last molecule what I would have expected." What we expect emerges from the world of words that Lewis built. The "expository *daemon,*" as Lewis called it, simply a synonym for "genius," took charge, and we get that brilliantly rich composition that was Lewis's career as scholar, story-teller, and apologist. From that mix of innate ability, rhetorical temper, suffering and delay, and astonishing will there emerged the utterly prepossessing man of letters.

II

"Letters" means language and its deployment, about which Lewis had thought much. In "Bluspels and Flalansferes," Lewis discusses the origin, nature, and function of language, a discussion based almost entirely on the metaphor, that agent which provokes the imagination and carries the intermediary image between language and apprehension. Lewis's point, like the great I. A. Richards's in *Principles of Literary Criticism*, is that all language is metaphorical, whether the particular metaphor is dead or alive. Few of Lewis's books are more heavily annotated than his Richards's *Principles of Literary Criticism*, a copy of which Richards inscribed to Lewis, saying that if he had read the annotations before writing the book, then he would have written a very different book. In a marginal annotation of Richards's idea that consciousness is a result of our "feeling" satisfactory and unsatisfactory neural changes, and which would become a footnote in *The Abolition of Man*, Lewis remarks, "if value = satisfaction why increase consciousness, that is, increase the power of having both satisfactions and dissatisfactions?" After describing how metaphors, the verbal instruments of consciousness, are either found or, for the sake of explanation, made, he convincingly demonstrates that all language is a function of our concept of space and time.

But Rudolph Steiner's Anthroposophy made no distinction between the material and the immaterial with regard to the function of imagination. Steiner held "the established belief that everything around us is bewitched spiritual truth, and that man attains truth when he breaks the spell." Thus, say, fairy tales do not simply convey or express truth but are the truth, in a disguised form. Lewis, rejecting the Anthroposophical contention that primitive consciousness did not distinguish between who is doing the looking and what is being looked at, nevertheless allowed that metaphor, symbol, and myth reflect truth: "I do not think the resemblance between the Christian and the merely imaginative experience is accidental":

Imagination, producing new metaphors or revivifying old, is not the cause of truth, but its condition. It is, I confess, undeniable that such a view indirectly implies a kind of truth or rightness in the imagination itself. I said at the outset that the truth we won by metaphor could not be greater than the truth of the metaphor itself; and . . . all our truth, or all but a few fragments, is won by metaphor. And thence, I confess, it does follow that if our thinking is ever true, then the metaphors by which we think must have been good metaphors. It does follow that . . . if there is not, in fact, a kind of psycho-physical parallelism (or more) in the universe then all our thinking is nonsensical. The life of the imagination is lower than the life of the spirit, but the former still retains the shape of the latter, the reality it reflects.

The important point is that metaphors should be recognized as such. Our thought is independent of the metaphors we employ only in so far as these metaphors are optional, "that is, in so far as we are able to have the same idea without them . . . . On the other hand, where the metaphor is our only method of reaching a given idea at all, there our thinking is limited by the metaphor so long as we retain the metaphor; and when the metaphor becomes fossilized, our thinking" is not thinking at all. At best, we have no more than a choice from among many metaphors, an *imaginative* choice. (On this and many related points I refer the reader to Doris T. Myers's allusive, penetrating, and definitive *C. S. Lewis in Context*, which lives up to its title, and more.) The imaginative experience, then, is what the artist avails himself of when he makes his poem, and makes it communicable. "For me," Lewis wrote, "reason is the natural organ of truth; but imagination is the organ of meaning," an idea both medieval and Anthroposophical.

"Rightness" is often conveyed as myth, which Lewis hastily defined as "an account of what *may have been* historical fact." This supposition has its roots in metaphor and appeals to the imagination. In *An Experiment in Criticism,* he says that because myth can take almost any form and deal with almost any "subject," it must be defined by its effect upon the receiver, which is invariably profound, momentous, everlasting, and numinous; though sad or joyful, it is always grave and, odd though it sounds, human sympathy is at a minimum. It almost always deals with fantastic characters or events and because it lacks the usual narrative attractions (e.g., suspense and complication) is extra-literary. In "Shelley, Dryden, and Mr. Eliot," Lewis summarizes: "Myth is thus like manna; it is to each man a different dish and to each the dish he needs. It does not grow old nor stick at frontiers racial, sexual, or philosophic; and even from the same man at the same moment it can elicit different responses at different levels."

Whence this power? That is, what ultimate rightness do symbol, metaphor, and myth—as mediated by the imagination—possess? Authors from the Romantic period to the present have seen it, but Lewis has insisted upon it with absolute clarity and conviction. Throughout his work, Lewis makes this connection clear: There is a supernature. All mythologies have some truth insofar as they embody elements of the Christian mythology, and this is so because, as Lewis entitled an essay, "Myth became Fact," that Fact was Jesus Christ. In *The Pilgrim's Regress,* John the Pilgrim hears a voice in the moment of his baptism: "'Child, if you will, it *is* mythology. It is but truth, not fact: an image, not the very real. But then it is My mythology. The words of Wisdom are also myth and metaphor. . . . But this is My inventing, this is the veil under which I have chosen to appear even from the first until now. For this end I made your senses and for this end your imagination, that you might see My Face and live.'"

Let us try our own experiment, for example, with *Perelandra*. Is it a myth? What follows is my own rendition, a bare-boned summary that should satisfy Lewis's requirements if the tale is mythic.

> On the planet Perelandra—a beautiful Paradise of water, floating islands, and Fixed Land—there dwelt a Green Lady and her King. Maleldil, Maker of All Things, gave them all they could want, but he forbade them ever to remain on the Fixed Land during night. The Green Lady and the King returned Maleldil's love and obeyed Him. Then it happened that the Lady and the King became separated. At that time the Dark Power of Earth, enemy of Maleldil and of all His creatures, came to the Lady. He tried to persuade her to disobey Maleldil, and he might have succeeded had not Ransom, one of Maleldil's loyal servants from Earth, intervened. In spite of the danger to himself and at the cost of great suffering, Ransom fought the Dark Power and drove him into the Deep. And so it came to pass that the Green Lady and the King, because they had not disobeyed Maleldil, were raised to high glory as the Father and Mother of a new beginning.

Profound, numinous, and grave—only the reader can say, and the response may vary from reader to reader. Yet to be compelling the tale ought to be, not only mythic, but probable as well. Ransom's observations and reactions would surely be our own if . . . ? That *if* is the key word. Reality, poetry, imagination, concreteness—each of these is, ultimately, dependent for its expression, use, or effectiveness on likely and probable *ifs*. *If* you are writing a story, Lewis tells us in *Miracles*, his defense of these phenomena, abnormal events may be bad art, or they may not. If, for example, you are writing an ordinary realistic novel and have got your characters into a hopeless muddle, it would be quite intolerable if you suddenly cut the knot and secured a happy ending by having a fortune left to the hero from an unexpected quarter. On the other hand there is nothing against taking as your subject from the outset adventures of a man who inherits an unexpected fortune. The unusual event is perfectly permissible if it is what you are really writing about.

In a letter Lewis revealed that *Perelandra* does indeed work out a supposition: What *if* there were an unspoiled paradise undergoing some temptation? What *if* angels were like unto the pagan gods? What if? Why, then we would have *Perelandra*.

In a letter to a child, Lewis advised never to use abstract nouns when concrete ones would do and that description should always replace "telling" adjectives; responses should be elicited, not pleaded for, thus to increase the sense of probability. "Poetry is an exploitation of language to convey the concrete," as with Ransom's first experience of the young planet:

> His first impression was nothing more definite than of something slanted—as though he were looking at a photograph which had been taken when the camera was not held level. And even this lasted only for an instant. The slant was replaced by a different slant; then two slants rushed together and made a peak, and the peak flattened suddenly into a horizontal line, and the horizontal line tilted and made and became the edge of a vast gleaming slope which rushed furiously towards him. At the same moment he felt that he was being lifted. Up and up he soared till it seemed as if he must reach the burning dome of gold that hung above him instead of a sky

.... As he rushed smoothly up the great convex hillside of the next wave he got a mouthful of water.... Though he had not been aware of his thirst till now, his drink gave him quite astonishing pleasure. It was almost like meeting Pleasure itself for the first time.... There was a wave ahead of him now so high it was dreadful.... He turned round .... Far down below him in a vast momentary valley he saw the thing that had missed him. It was variegated in colours like a patch-work quilt—flame colour, ultramarine, crimson, orange, gamboge, and violet.

The multi-sensory images seem perfectly ordered, requiring of the reader an attentive submission, virtually an active participation. The reward is that the reader feels he has been there, right along with Ransom.

And what is more probable than Ransom trying to rationalize his presence on Perelandra? What is more likely than that he should find a false security in his casuistic conclusion? And what is more probable than that at this very moment of putative triumph all his reasoning should break to pieces? And *if*—God forbid—any of us ever meets a devil, will he not be exactly as Lewis portrays him? Or have we already seen them in any evil that walks the earth?

It looked at Ransom in silence and at last began to smile. We have all spoken—Ransom himself had often spoken— of a devilish smile. Now he realized that he had never taken the words seriously. The smile was not bitter, nor raging, nor, in any ordinary sense, sinister; it was not even mocking. It seemed to summon Ransom, with horrible naïveté of welcome, into the world of its own pleasures, as if all men were at one in those pleasures, as if they were the most natural thing in the world and no dispute could ever have occurred about them. It was not furtive, nor

ashamed, it had nothing of the conspirator in it. It did
not defy goodness, it ignored it to the point of annihi-
lation.

This suggestion of "what might have been historical fact," in
the midst of concrete images and a self-consistent plot, offers
the kind of experience which takes the reader out of himself.
That self has been elsewhere, is shaken, and so occupies new
ground. The worthy text casts a spell. If its quiddity, the very
thingness of the thing, is submitted to, then that otherness
compels a reader to enjoy the object and avoid self-regard.

III

In addition to myth and probability, the *sort* of spell must
matter greatly if a healthy and disinterested journey is to be
undertaken, for both good spells and bad have been known
to get results. In *The Allegory of Love,* Lewis suggests the right
sort, drawing a persevering distinction. Allegory results when
we invent *visibilia*—characters such as Patience, Wrath, or
Lewis's own Giant in *The Pilgrim's Regress*—to represent immaterial facts, such as passions. But, Lewis continues,

> there is another way of using the equivalence, which is
> almost the opposite of allegory, and which I would call
> sacramentalism or symbolism. If our passions, being im-
> material, can be copied by material inventions, then it is
> possible that our material world in its turn is the copy
> of an invisible world. . . . The allegorist leaves the given—
> his own passions—to talk of that which is confessedly
> less real, which is a fiction. The symbolist leaves the given
> to find that which is more real. To put the difference in
> another way, for the symbolist it is we who are the alle-
> gory.

We should not believe that allegory does not reveal reality, for in *Reflections on the Psalms,* Lewis tells us precisely the opposite. But it is sacramentalism that carries the real power. Lewis maintains that "it is for most poets and in most poems by far the best method of writing poetry which is religious without being devotional." A close, and personal, look at what may be his greatest single achievement, *The Chronicles of Narnia,* I think illustrates the point, illustrating as well Lewis's great synthesizing, imaginative genius.

During a graduate school summer of 1968, eating badly, sleeping little, and losing weight, I was blessed with the worst cold I have ever had. Now—and in good conscience—I could actually stop working. I could even stay in bed for days. A dark, heavy rain fell steadily, insulating me in my seclusion as I lay close by an open window enjoying my favorite weather. What to do, when not sleeping away the day or listening to baseball games late at night? Although I had read very much of Lewis, I had by no means read all that was available, and though a life-long reader of faerie, I had curiously put off reading *The Chronicles of Narnia,* which just now seemed perfectly suited to the circumstances. So for five days I read the seven *Chronicles,* drinking in all I could of their danger, heroism, and merriment, which both quenched and aroused a great thirst. I had never before been taken so utterly out of myself to that reality-right-around-the-corner, perpetually new, awful, rampant, true, and good. C. S. Lewis was already to me what Chesterton had been to him, but now he would be my MacDonald, too. For what else does Narnia do but "baptize the imagination"?

Since then I have read the series, as such, several times, though never in any of the two or three prescribed orders; and I have read my favorites, *The Magician's Nephew, The Silver*

Chair, and *The Last Battle*) many more times than that. Yet here is a curious fact: I cannot remember them quite as I do almost everything else I have read of Lewis's. And it does not seem to matter. Having avoided "studies" of Narnia whenever possible, I also avoid studying them myself. Thus, instead of remembering Narnian chronology, or the names of the three sleeping lords, or even the four signs, I revisit characters and scenes, summoning up images, moods, tone, and "flavor." I very greatly enjoy but only reluctantly contemplate. That is, I know Narnia as most of us know ourselves and our own lives, much more by *connaître* than by *savoir*.

Of course, even such a reader wonders about Narnia-the-literary-creation, especially about the sources and nature of its allure. If wondering out loud, he might offer up "a dish of orts," as George MacDonald might have it, not entirely unappetizing, though assuredly personal and lacking in novelty. My own questions are not only old but simple: What are *The Chronicles of Narnia*? How do they work? Toward what end are they directed? To answer them I would take as my starting point a thoroughly Lewisian premise: The imagination, when kindled by a beam of sacramental longing, encounters holiness. That is its baptism; and that is precisely the "dialectic of desire" that Narnia seems to occasion. With nothing less than our spiritual destiny at stake, its Joy calls us home. Here is where the regressing pilgrim asks how and why it is that Narnia breaks his heart.

The first premise invites a second, both Lewisian and pronouncedly Christian. The road home begins behind a thick, heavily-bolted door marked "self"; so the regressing pilgrim is also a fugitive. The *Chronicles*, then, for the part they play in the breakout, are "escapist." That is, they educe, "draw out, elicit." In *Beyond Words: Mystical Fancy in Children's Literature,*

James E. Higgins writes that no one "has to remind parents that bad books can seduce. Are they as alert to books which can educe the inner, unique, individual child?" Thus "escapist" or eductive books are the ones which best serve our spiritual destiny—to enter the kingdom of heaven; better than others they lead us out of ourselves "as little children."

To effect this transformation in his readers (be they big or little), Lewis relies upon such figures as giants, dwarfs, and talking beasts, which he considered hieroglyphs, for gruffness, shyness, and the like. He writes fairy tales, the best of all eductive literature, because they deal with "a spiritual universe," Higgins continues, "the unfathomable, awesome meaning of life to which age and maturity fail to bring one closer." This is why Lewis, who believed that "a book no longer worth reading by an adult was never worth reading in the first place," wrote with children in mind; "fairy stories say"—and do—"best what's to be said"—and done to and for all who would flee as little children. For those who would not, may Susan serve as a warning. At Aslan's rising she asks "How?" She would be grown-up and understand. Finally, like some of the dwarfs at the end of *The Last Battle*, she remembers her self, only herself, and elects not to be fooled, not to "play silly games." So she remains in prison, suffering from "ignorance of fairyland," as Higgins puts it, "the vanity of too many adults who have forgotten that education is leading forth, not stuffing in."

The *Chronicles* seem to be a perfect marriage between form and function, mystical fancy, as Higgins puts it, and escapism, or eduction. At least that is the judgment of a reader who removes himself from Narnia and assumes the role of literary analyst. From within the world, where he belongs, that reader sees things differently. He stands slightly above the children as they encounter the Narnian creator face-to-face and discovers along with them many of the supernatural workings of that world; from this point-of-view he reads *theogony*, how the gods begin. If the reader shifts his perspective to that of many of the Narnian creatures, yet another form emerges: the appearance of gods and of God in the everyday world and their participation in the world that is the stuff of *theophany*. What else—for a Narnian, that is—do these stories chronicle? This mix of elements—mystical fancy, eduction, theogony, and theophany—add up to a sacred scripture, an emblem of the Scriptures themselves (as Charles Huttar has suggested). This is what Lewis means by literary sacramentalism.

There are as many ways of accounting for a literary work as there are critical methodologies. Underlying all of them is this piece of common reader's sense from Kenneth Grahame, the author of one of Lewis's favorites, *The Wind in the Willows*, and a writer who ought to know: "Vitality, that is the test; and whatever its components mere fact is not necessary. A dragon, for instance, is a more enduring animal than a pterodactyl. I have never yet met anyone who really believed in a pterodactyl; but every honest person believes in dragons— down in the back kitchen of his consciousness." This idea of belief *in*, not belief *that*, makes all the difference. Eustace believed that a star is a ball of flaming gas, but he did not believe in stars—until he met one. Lewis understood this distinction, of course, and possessed the talent to render his world so vital that most submissive readers, and some not so submissive, cannot help believing in that world.

More important, however, than understanding or even than talent in eliciting this kind of belief was Lewis's ability to lend it himself. For example, he seems really to have believed in Tommy, the pet mouse to whom he wrote in 1907, in Mr. Papworth, the dog whom he had to feed over his shoul-

der, without looking back, and in Bultitude, the Whipsnade
Zoo bear, with the same sort of conviction that we lend to the
jackdaw who is the first joke in *The Magician's Nephew,*
Reepicheep, the gay and martial mouse, and to Aslan himself.
The heart of them—their quiddity, or hieroglyphic significance—never seemed to escape him. (Lewis's talkative raven
is as the great naturalist Konrad Lorenz described his raven
to be in *King Solomon's Ring,* a book we know Lewis to have
read and liked.) His primary imagination unfailingly distin-
guished that which an object *is* from that of which it is *made,*
connaître from *savoir,* "belief in" from "belief that." This faculty—an immensely capacious "organ of meaning"—is what
occasions such insights as "dog plus man closes a gap in the
universe" and (in a letter to a child who asked why God made
dogs for us) "perhaps God made us for dogs," or Narnian vitality itself.

This feature of conviction applies, as well, to the nature
or essence of the Narnian cosmos which is posited as much
as it is rendered. Once assented to, it becomes the condition
of nearly all other "belief in." As Lewis puts it, "the *plot,* as we
call it, is only really a net whereby to catch something else.
The real theme may be . . . something that has no sequence
in it, something other than a process and much more like a
state or quality." It seems ineffable. We discern it most readily
by way of the strange familiarity—or is it the familiar strangeness?—of the Narnian creatures. Fauns, satyrs, unicorns, giants, dwarfs, dryads, witches, and a flying horse turn out to
be more than hieroglyphs and much more than the allegorical figures complained about by Tolkien when he heard it read
at the Inklings. Rather, they are mnemonic stimuli—like
musical chords, or a smell, or the pattern on a fabric—calling to mind something we once knew, believed in, and very

much liked, but have since forgotten. Though in perfect keeping with castles, courtesy, kings, and other medieval accou-
trement, they are more than mere trappings. The something
they call to mind is a *mode of perception*, a something far more
medieval than the hieroglyphs themselves.

"Man loves as he sees," wrote Angela of Foligno, a mystic, and "the vision of this world," continues Carolly Erickson
in *The Medieval Vision*, was "linked to the vision of the next,"
ours being a "graphic model of the continuous act of creation"
and "conceived as embracing the geographical locus of un-
seen truths." The difference between Narnia and our world, and
between the historical medieval vision and our own, is in
precisely this view of the here-and-now. We have forgotten
that it points to, compels us towards, and derives from the then-
and-elsewhere. In Narnia, the voyagers on the *Dawn Treader*—
like the medieval Mesopotamian monks who traveled to the
East—could find a place where heaven meets earth. This link-
ing of worlds, and our ability to discern the next one in this,
is at the heart of the Narnian drama, from the ringing of the
bell in Charn to the triumphant gallop following the last battle.
This is sacramentalism to the core, for in it "God . . . appears
frequently but always *incognito*," as Jesus did. This world figures
the next; the *Chronicles* figure that very process of figuring.
Narnia mediates reality; the *Chronicles* compel us to see and
to know by way of mediation. Such is the "state or quality"
of this world, and as such ought we to believe *in* it.

One of the ends of the *Chronicles*, then, is to fix our attention on a *means* of surpassing importance: a mediating,
or symbolic, principle that invites us to see the next world in
this. "What I like about experience," said Lewis, "is that it is
such an honest thing." The regressing pilgrim may have a
rough go of it, but he will prevail if he pays attention. Of course,

the sacramental nature of the world requires that he pay attention to the right thing—if Joy is to baptize his imagination and prove a reliable guide. "Only when your whole attention and desire are fixed on something else," continues Lewis, "whether a distant mountain, or the past, or the gods of Asgard"—or the creatures and events of Narnia—"does the 'thrill' arise. It [Joy, of course] is a by-product."

This "law of inattention," to call it by a paradoxical but I think accurate name, requires of a literary work that it be, like the world it imitates, oblique, sometimes even inverted, as is the case with *The Great Divorce*, from one direction, and with *The Silver Chair*, from the other. This is why Lewis and others are so strict about stealing past those "watchful dragons" of self-consciousness or of formulaic interpretation when reading. In *A Dish of Orts*, George MacDonald writes that the meaning of a fairy tale, unlike that of an allegory, may be different for each reader, but that it "cannot help having some meaning if it have proportion and harmony it has vitality, and vitality is truth." With a common touch equal to Kenneth Grahame's, MacDonald adds that if a horse needs a label, it is a badly drawn horse. As much to the point is Tzvetan Todorov's *The Fantastic: A Structuralist Approach to a Literary Genre* as a defense of literary fantasy, a mode of perception particularly effective at instilling belief in the reader and at achieving an equilibrium between two worlds, so that in the lesser of the two there is "nothing arbitrary." In examining point-of-view, Todorov concludes that a fantasy protagonist is especially suited to standing in for the reader, for the character hesitates between the natural and the supernatural, ultimately partaking of both.

So we readers of Narnia are to be see-ers and knowers; we are to see by mediation, knowing the next world in this.

Because the worlds are linked sacramentally, that knowing is of the right sort—*connaître*. We must pay attention—remember, inattention leaves some inexperienced all their lives—even though the object of our attention communicate merely obliquely. Lewis realized, as Paul Holmer puts it in *C. S. Lewis: The Shape of His Faith and Thought*, that "becoming a knower supposes a readiness to see" and that seeing articulates capabilities. Lewis's people are subjects, not objects ("You can't study people, you can only get to know them"); so how the animals and children live "determines what they love and finally even know. . . . a frame of life and mind within which some things become accessible to us."

The children in *Prince Caspian* perfectly exemplify the symbolic importance of the fantasy protagonist. Upon arriving in Narnia they are confused, even lost. Before remembering who and what they are, they must know where they are; this knowledge, though, is preceded by a dawning consciousness, a recognition of an altered state of being. (Even their stature and physical prowess are enhanced.) They are gods—or angels—once again and know themselves as such. The children (and we, for they establish our point-of-view) see "theogonically." If Narnia may be visited sacramentally, may we not be so visited as well? There opens to us a "frame of life and mind" suggesting that there is indeed "nothing arbitrary" about our world, though it reveals itself "by implication only." The *Chronicles* figure forth a world on the brink, a theatrical set (to paraphrase Lewis—and Chesterton) about to become the real thing—a transposition in which we (our children-surrogates) will have a hand.

Now we here can "read" the mediating illusions; living is an interpretive, critical enterprise. Once you know that there are signs—symbols, hieroglyphs, "spilled religion"—then you may infer, unless you are a mystic, which Lewis certainly was not, some Elsewhere from which they derive. As usual, Lewis puts it more pointedly, in "Is Theology Poetry?": "The waking world is judged more real because it can thus contain the dreaming worlds; the dreaming world is judged less real because it cannot contain the waking one. For the same reason I am certain that in passing from the scientific point of view [*savoir*?] to the theological, I have passed from dream to waking. . . . I believe in Christianity as I believe the sun has risen not only because I see it but because by it I see everything else." In fact, *The Silver Chair* is hardly about anything except knowing: knowing the signs, paying attention, recollecting, distrusting the absolute claims of mere fact. Its evil, as we encounter it in Underworld, is "the decay of true knowledge," as John D. Cox so aptly puts it in "Epistemological Release in *The Silver Chair*." Only in Aslan's country—where all harms are healed—are the highest claims, especially that of certainty, affirmed.

Lewis knew, esteemed, recommended, and used two books that come particularly to the point. The first is Edwyn Bevan's *Symbolism and Belief*; the second, Rudolph Otto's *The Idea of the Holy*. The former provides a thorough and coherent rationale for Lewis's method in the *Chronicles*, so much so that one wonders if he had it open at his elbow as he wrote them. (Bevan's examination of Philo's advice to avoid a "direct frontal approach" to God is especially interesting.) The latter, though, addresses the point of affirmation, the last and highest point. What do we come to know, however obliquely? What is it that works the wonder of baptism upon the imagination? Lewis's answer is Holiness, or, as Otto puts it, the *mysterium tremendum*, the *mysterium fascinosum*, and the *numinous*: the fathomless mystery attaching to the sacred being, the deep enchantment of the worshipper as he contemplates that being, and his accompanying awe and fear before the sacred, respectively. In short, the source of all affirmations, Affirmation Himself.

If we are to "become as little children," then it is not surprising that one leads us best. As some of the voyagers from the ship *Dawn Treader* move through "drinkable light" (an image closely resembling one Lewis had used in an early short story, "The Man Born Blind"), they realize that they are approaching, like those medieval travelers, the end of the world, the end of Narnia. It requires Lucy—who else could it be?—to know that such an end is an end of obliqueness only. The hieroglyphs, signs, symbols, and sacraments are a means to that to which the *Chronicles* direct us. "'It isn't Narnia, you know,' sobbed Lucy. 'It's you. We shan't meet you'" back in our world. "'And how can we live, never meeting you?'" As we all know, Aslan reassures Lucy, and then sends us all back, out of the world figured forth by C. S. Lewis and into a world—our very own mediating illusion—figured forth by our Creator: "This was the very reason why you were brought to Narnia, that by knowing me here for a little, you may know me better there."

5

Rhetoric

Rhetoric speaks to man in his whole being and out of his whole past and with reference to values which only a human being can intuit. . . . In the restored man dialectic and rhetoric will go along hand in hand as the regime of the human faculties intended that they should.

Richard Weaver
"The Cultural Role of Rhetoric"

I don't know if I'm weaker than other people, but it is a positive revelation to me how while the speech lasts *it is impossible not to waver just a little. I should be useless as a schoolmaster or a police-* man. *Statements which I* know *to be untrue all but convince me, at any rate for the moment, if only the man says them unflinchingly.*

C. S. Lewis,
after hearing a speech by Hitler,
the night before he conceived the idea
for *The Screwtape Letters*, July 21, 1940

C. S. LEWIS WOULD SEEM TO BE a one-man argument from design, for there is little in his life that is not of-a-piece, that does not have about it the feel of inevitability. His rhetorical temper provided a compulsiveness and a posture which could be resolved only in argument. Training, taste, and talent equipped him for an academic and apologetic career, to the exclusion of nearly all others, even the writing of poetry, especially his beloved narrative poetry, at which he had no more than minor success. Of course, he could not have remained an atheist, in his case rather an aberration than a settled state; so his conversion added direction to the high purpose towards which he had turned his will. Apparently, he could think, read, and write twice as much as most people, but in half the time. His attentiveness, hermeneutic vigor, and memory, not to mention his raw intellectual power make his life seem "thicker" than most. "Inattention leaves some inexperienced all their lives," he wrote. But not Lewis. Where but to life—that is, to thought, reading, and experience—would he turn when looking for *topoi*, the "places" for argument, his subject matter, suitable as the raw material of his invention? His geniuses applied his own pain, grief, doubt, sin, wonder, appreciation, lessons, and learning, evidencing not some shallow facility but a triumph of charity, and the fact that he, not the scavenged, half-understood, misrepresented celebrity, could make it look so easy allows it to seem possible for the rest of us.

Because it was lived through, Lewis's variegated, organic, and concrete "thickness" of experience has the ring of authenticity, and so it bestows, or uncovers, or illuminates, meaning over a vast range of work. Not all of the terrain is equally inviting to every reader; but each is bound to find something congenial, then something else, and then perhaps a third thing, and so on. The expedition becomes exciting, for each explorer begins to feel as though he were discovering things on his own. The trick, of course, is to get people to stop and stroll in the first place. The taste and texture of another landscape may be constant, but its realization in concrete rhetorical art must be adaptive, many-faceted; for not everyone recognizes, or even prefers, the same pathways in any given territory. Indeed, many prefer not to be taken "right out of the self" at all. Given our tendency to stand guard over ourselves, to contemplate our responses rather than to enjoy them, any amount of "smuggling," by whatever channels, must be undertaken. In his maturity, Lewis wastes nothing—no discovery; neither taste, nor talent, nor preference. So after the outburst of *The Pilgrim's Regress* the power is harnessed; he gets down to business.

And that business grows and branches out, just like a tree. From annotation to notebook, from notebook to essay or address, from address to one sort of book, from one sort of book to another—from one way of knowing to another— Lewis and his world of discourse form a coherent whole, a tapestry of meaning. In believing that Christ intends for us to be persons (members of His Person), Lewis uses the occasion to offer his audience recognizable fragments of personality and to show them what those fragments might become. Having taken seriously the claim that the universe is possessed of meaning, he then provides an image of reality sufficiently coherent and authoritative to make the claim credible. Paul Holmer, in *C. S. Lewis: The Shape of His Faith and Thought*, perhaps the best book on Lewis, writes that

> He shows us repeatedly... how a kind of moral certitude is finally achieved. He sends us back to our fathers, mothers, nurses, poets, sages, and lawgivers. The dignity he ascribes to all of us is exceedingly flattering.... The

tissue of life around us, when taken with seriousness, is already a moral order. We have to become its qualified readers. . . . The world has no single character, and it must be understood in a variety of ways. His books create, almost as Kierkegaard did, the living variety of paradigms . . . . Here the requirements are new capabilities, new capacities altogether . . . For his works, especially the novels, have a way of creating a kind of longing for innocence, for purity, for humility, candor, and contentment. . . . Only its occasion can be created by another, and that is what Lewis's literature becomes. Wisdom has to be read off the whole shape of his thought and is not one trick within it.

I

Near the beginning of the second book of his *Metaphysics,* Aristotle instructs us that "those who wish to succeed must ask the right preliminary questions." The two never asked of Lewis are, What is he? and How ought we to "read" him? I have been contending that the "algorithm" at once most revealing and parsimonious is rhetorical, those subsets of questions and lines of inquiry deriving from Aristotle's definition of rhetoric: *The faculty of observing in the* particular *case the available means of persuasion.* Forty-five years ago, one of our most respected rhetorical theorists, Donald C. Bryant, wrote that "what Aristotle said of the nature and principles of public address, of the discovery of all the available means of persuasion in any given case, must stand as the broad background for a sensible rhetorical system."

The conception of rhetoric that emerged from Aristotle and others is that of a series of systematic adjustments among purpose, circumstances, and strategies. Those circumstances are marked by "exigencies," urgent problems that demand a resolution by persuasion. There are constraints, of course, inherent to any occasion, the most restrictive being the limitations of what Aristotle called the "judge," any audience empowered to mediate a resolution. To these circumstances the communicator brings his resources. Some of these are ready made, such as his reputation, and others are discovered, or "invented," to address the question at hand, for example some bit of refutation that responds to an objection, or a definition unique to the subject at hand.

Together these elements make up the tactics and strategy of a given persuasive effort. What proofs could the communicator bring to bear? They could be of three types. Logical proof combines evidence with reasoning and leads to some conclusion based upon some established premise, or "warrant." Emotional proof, sometimes called "pathetic" proof—from the Greek word *pathe*, a state which gives rise to a particular feeling—arouses and directs passion, either muted and subtle or demonstrative. Personal proof is the third and last type; sometimes called "ethical" proof—from the Greek word *ethos*, character—and derives from the communicator *per se*. We think of it as trustworthiness or "charisma." Respectively, these three proofs dwell within the discourse (the speech, book, article, sermon, election campaign, television commercial, and the like), the audience, and the communicator.

The rhetorician then "discovers" the proofs best suited to the circumstances, including the exigency, audience, medium of communication, time limit, location, and occasion. Next he organizes them; then he formulates them. These three stages are known as "invention" (which means to uncover or to discover, not "to make up"), "disposition" (the putting of something into its proper place), and style (usually verbal but actually referring to the overall flavor of the presentation). The fourth and fifth "canons," or functions, that the rhetorician undertakes are preparation (what we think of as rehearsal) and, at last, delivery. Underlying the process is the concept of *topos*, or "place." These are standard ideas, conceptions, or arguments that can be applied, with appropriate modification, to the *particular* case at hand, or the characteristic bases of a particular rhetorician's arguments. For example, every murder case raises the questions of the motive, means, and opportunity of the accused; these *topoi*, or topics, as we call them, are then applied to the circumstances of *this* murder and to *this* defendant. Finally, preferences in style have varied widely over the millennia, but for the last century or so ours has been for the plain style: some figures of speech—metaphors, analogies and the like—but not too many verbal ornaments that approach poetry. In other words, we prefer rhetoric that is an extension of natural, direct conversation.

Of overriding importance is the nature of rhetoric as an inherent faculty—an ability to make or to do, like the imagination or the memory—of any human being: an ineluctable feature of everyone's interior landscape. We are constantly persuading ourselves, as Craig R. Smith puts it in his *Rhetoric and Human Consciousness: A History*, and the way we persuade ourselves, noted Aristotle, is the way we persuade others. Rhetoric is also *epistemic*; it has a "making known" function, suggesting probabilities and therefore helping us to make decisions. As the great classical scholar George A. Kennedy has shown, in his *Comparative Rhetoric: An Historical and Cross-Cultural Introduction*, all cultures practice rhetoric and have, or have had, characteristic "rhetorics," styles of persuasion that emerge from their particular history, customs, mores, and expectations. In short, Aristotle could have begun his seminal *On Rhetoric* with the words, "all people by nature love to, and must, rhetorize." If Lewis had been around, he would have been Aristotle's model.

Yet, if rhetoric was the prime minister of Lewis's parliament of geniuses, he nevertheless found its classical lineaments and post-classical emphases entirely uncongenial. What he apparently never fathomed, although it is impossible to imagine that he did not know it, was the Greek's definition of the art as a *faculty*. "Rhetoric is the greatest barrier"—surely this is Lewis's greatest exaggeration—"between us and our ancestors. If the Middle Ages had erred in their devotion to that art, the *renascentia*, far from curing, confirmed the error." In his Oxford literary history, he continues with a description of the antiquity and enormous influence of rhetoric, noting its unbroken continuity into the eighteenth century, "not the tyrant, but the darling of humanity, *soavissima*, as Dante says, 'the sweetest of all the other sciences'."

Lewis acknowledges that our older poetry was written by people who knew no distinction between poetry and rhetoric and that they praised "beauties" at best opaque to us. "This change of taste makes an invisible wall between us and them. Probably all our literary histories, *certainly that on which I am engaged*, are vitiated by our lack of sympathy on this point [emphasis added]." What follows is a description of a system of education based upon the devoted study of figures of speech and of thought (which even today not everyone finds tiresome), the universal enthusiasm for that education, which Lewis compares to a modern schoolboys concern about "county cricketers or types of aeroplanes," and its efficacy: "They talk something like angels and something like sailors and stableboys; never like civil servants or writers of leading articles." Let it not pass unnoticed that Lewis attributes his own antipathy to just about everyone who would read his book.

Lewis's discussions and depictions of the art are straight-forward. The scholar treats of it at length in three places: *English Literature in the Sixteenth Century*, *The Discarded Image: An Introduction to Medieval and Renaissance Literature*, and *A Preface to Paradise Lost*. In the second he provides a dazzling summary of medieval rhetorical theory—thorough, full of telling detail, and replete with apt examples, mostly from Chaucer. Of particular interest here is Lewis's attention to one Geoffrey of Vinsauf, whose *Nove Poetria* of the early thirteenth century achieved commanding influence. It is precisely the sort of rhetoric that would vex Lewis, but the vexation does not show in his description. In his *Preface to Paradise Lost*, Lewis exhibits his most impressive grasp of rhetoric, respond-ing to the oldest of all the indictments against it:

> First, as to Manipulation. I do not think (and no great civilization has ever thought) that the art of the rheto-rician is necessarily vile. It is in itself noble. . . . Both [rhetoric and poetry] aim at doing something to an au-dience. And both do it by using language to control what already exists in our minds. . . . The differentia of Rhetoric is that it wishes to produce some practical resolve. . . and it does this by calling passion to the aid of reason. . . . The proper use is lawful and necessary because, as Aristotle points out, intellect of itself "moves nothing": the transition from thinking to doing. . . needs to be assisted by appropriate states of feeling. Because the end of Rhetoric is in the world of action, the objects it deals with appear foreshortened and much of their reality is omitted. . . . Very roughly, we might almost say that in Rhetoric imagination is present for the sake of passion (and, therefore, in the long run, for the sake of action), while in poetry passion is present for the sake of imagi-nation, and therefore, in the long run, for the sake of wisdom or spiritual health. . . .

—that is, *psychagogia*. Notwithstanding his caveat about his own lack of sympathy, this thumbnail definition of rhetoric is among the very best I have ever read. In a small number of letters and very short articles, Lewis gives rhetorical advice; in scholarly works he describes the art, provides some history, and renders disinterested judgment.

II

Strictly speaking, an advocate who takes the initiative is simply a preacher or an expositor, but "you cannot well oppose the accusation of social disruptiveness without making a case for the cohesive tendencies of the gospel; you cannot clear the charge of silliness without establishing a claim to rationality. . . . The apologist's eye is on the point of attack. He is a frontiersman," as Austin Farrer reminds us. Accordingly, the Judeo-Christian tradition of apologetics is characterized, says the *New Catholic Encyclopedia*, closely echoing St. Augustine in Book IV of his *De Doctrina Christiana*, by God's "self-disclosure. . . in the contemporary world," concerning itself with "the relationship between faith and reason." Thus "the apologetic attempt is to persuade, *to translate*, in the literal sense, the Christian demand for faith (emphasis added)."

Not all preaching is necessarily apologetic, of course, but all (Christian) apologetic has about it an aspect of preaching. Karl Barth's *Homiletics* outlines "The Criteria of the Sermon," all of which are applicable to Lewis and most of which he satisfies most of the time:

1. Revelation: immersion in and proclamation of the Word of Jesus;

2. Church: in Barth's view a reformulation of Mere Christianity;

3. Confession: the response one makes to what he has heard;

4. Ministry: the special responsibility to answer a calling;

5. Holiness: the sanctification of a sinner who, speaking under the law, has faith in the promise of divine blessing;

6. Scripture: not a "welling up of our own speech" but an exposition of Revelation (or, as Lewis put it, not "my religion");

7. Originality: the breaking through of Scripture in a spirit of repentance and thankfulness that warrants the preacher's own words and thinking;

8. Congregation: aiming at people in a specific time, place, and set of circumstances; and

9. Spirituality: the soulful and prayerful realization that "God himself must confess their human word if it is to be God's word" (a variation of St. Francis de Sales's injunction to place ourselves in the presence of God).

Lewis delivered only a handful of sermons, but they made history in their day. "Transposition" was delivered from the pulpit of Mansfield College, close to the house where Lewis stayed on his very first night in Oxford. "The Weight of Glory" and "Learning in War-Time" were preached to multitudes from the pulpit of the University Church of St. Mary the Virgin. Lattimer, Cranmer, and Ridley had been tried there; Wesley, Keble, and Newman preached from the same pulpit. (The church is just down High Street from number 36, Williams Hairdresser, a visit to which occasioned "The Efficacy of

Prayer.") These are impressive venues. But as impressive in their variety and modesty are the venues of some of his greatest essays. Here is a sampling: *St. Jude's Gazette, World Dominion, Electrical and Musical Industries Christian Fellowship, Coventry Evening Telegraph, Bristol Diocesan Gazette, The Month, Breakthrough,* and *St. James's Magazine*; of course there were also *The Saturday Evening Post, The Guardian* (small but prominent in its day), *Time & Tide, Twentieth Century,* and *Spectator.* The subjects he treated were often the most difficult: If Jesus was God, why did he not return during the lifetime of those who actually heard him? If we are promised that prayers made faithfully will be answered, why are they so infrequently answered? If God is loving, why does he permit so much suffering, especially of the innocent—even of the beasts, who were not morally complicit in the Fall? What explanation other than psychosis could explain "speaking in tongues"? In the absence of evidence, why should we be "obstinate" in belief? How can we possibly reconcile dogmatic belief with the need freely to exercise our reason, presumably God-given?

Of the more than forty books Lewis published, all but some poetry and the works of literary scholarship and criticism are either argumentative defenses of Christian doctrine, explanations of it for the purpose of persuading in its favor, or manifestly didactic fictions with Christian intent; six have a veiled intent and the Christian content is submerged, but they fulfill precisely the same functions. This assessment applies even to *Till We Have Faces,* though as Lewis's one real novel (as opposed to parable, fairy tale, or romance) it differs considerably from its predecessors. The same is largely true of the books published posthumously. In many modes, at varying levels of intensity and directness, Lewis was relentlessly persuasive. The range of work—in its content, mode, scope, style, and persistence—is unremitting. Surely it came in stages, not unlike Lewis's life, and to some degree the stages of one echo those of the other. I will argue in the next chapter that the final three stages evidence the greatest alteration, after his conversion, in both his life and work, and for a particular reason. Now it is sufficient to note that, in its great array, the whole of his work speaks to a sufficient variety of tastes, intellectual abilities, religious doubts, spiritual needs, imaginative longings, and levels of curiosity to satisfy the preponderance of readers, no matter where they break in upon it. In his output Lewis comes as close as any to how the philosopher and rhetorician Richard Weaver describes the Complete Man: "The 'lover' added to the scientist; the rhetorician to the dialectician; understanding followed by actualization."

Among the most thoughtful appraisals of Lewis is this one from Debra Winger, the noted actress who so capably played the role of Joy Davidman in *Shadowlands*. Responding to a question that posited Lewis as a man who gave "easy" answers to "difficult questions"—a charge made promiscuously in the film—Winger, who in preparation had read much Lewis and Joy Davidman and had visited the Wade Center at Wheaton College, demurred. After avowing that she was not a Christian she told me, "He may make difficult *questions* accessible. I don't think he makes the answers 'easy.' I don't think he answers questions. I think he discusses them." She added that "He's in that school of discourse where his statements are not like books that are written by experts"; instead, she concluded, "He's saying 'think about this.' That's why I think he opened [Christianity] to so many people. He wasn't dogmatic." That is, in all its regions, Lewis's rhetoric is inseparable from his voice, both reasonable and rhapsodic, doubly inviting.

In a poem unpublished during his lifetime, Lewis adumbrates this view, calling more for integration and maturity than for redemption. In the last half of his sonnet "Reason," with Athene representing that faculty and Demeter the imagination, he writes,

> *Tempt not Athene. Wound not in her fertile pains*
> *Demeter, nor rebel against her mother-right.*
> *Oh who will reconcile in me both maid and mother,*
> *Who make in me a concord of the depth and height?*
> *Who make imagination's dim exploring touch*
> *Ever report the same as intellectual sight?*
> *Then could I truly say, and not deceive,*
> *Then wholly say, that I BELIEVE.*

More than merely Quintilian's "good man speaking well," this man who so seamlessly combined imagination and reason is a reliable guide to the things that matter most. It is of more than passing interest that "I believe," as Lewis would have known, is a loose translation of "Peitho," the Greek goddess of rhetoric, usually seen in the company of Aphrodite herself, the goddess of love.

III

Lewis certainly understood the demands of the art, discerning "the available means of persuasion," making astute choices, and adroitly deploying his resources. His characters are as subtle as the situation requires them to be, all the while remaining true to their limits. Lewis *depicts* rhetoric in all of his fictions. Frequently, speeches occur at important, even climactic, moments and evidence very sophisticated insight into rhetorical occasions and the varieties of discourse they engender. In *Perelandra* we see a debate between the hero, Ransom the philologist, and the Un-man, a human body animated by Evil itself. The planet Perelandra is still an unspoiled paradise, but its first Woman, who is witnessing the debate, may—depending upon the outcome of the debate—disobey a divine command and thus bring about her planet's Fall: argument and counter-argument will heavily influence her decision. In *The Great Divorce* people in a drab, dark, rain-soaked city—either Purgatory or Hell itself—take a bus trip to the fringe of Heaven, where they are met by very tangible spirits who seek to conduct them further in. There are several dramatic efforts at persuasion, some prolonged; all but one of the passengers (that we know of) return to the bus. Almost all of *Till We Have Faces* is a "forensic" speech—a formal accusation as though in a law court—casting blame upon the gods, who are "in the dock." (Queen Orual, the first-person narrator, has been tutored by a learned Greek slave known as the Fox but whose actual name is Lysias, a contemporary of Pericles and renowned ghostwriter and orator.

Lewis's world of discourse, excluding his work as a literary scholar, can be usefully construed as two concentric circles, a micro- and a macrocosmos. The smaller world invites a tactical analysis; the larger, a strategic one. But the distinction is not between short, expository works usually addressed to a highly particular audience and longer essays and fictions intended for a general readership. That association—short and local as the microcosmic, tactical realm; long, mimetic, or general, as the macrocosmic, strategic one—generally holds, but it does not define the distinction as much as reflect it. Very often, short, "particularized" works show strategic choices, just as long expositions and fictions often evidence tactical ones. The defining distinction is one of intellectual and rhetorical reach. That is, in any given work, just how much of his audience is Lewis attempting to compass? Are we expected to make two or three relatively simple ratiocinative moves, or is a deeper level of intellection—one on which we conceptualize, or examine heretofore hidden assumptions—required? Is passion called to aid reason, and, if so, is the object of that passion transcendent and perhaps eternal? Is the highest level of imagination aroused, so that we seem beckoned to travel, even to dwell, within another world altogether? In works both short and long, particularized and general, strictly expository and fictional, Lewis frequently attempts to reach both the lowest and the highest in his audience.

Paradigmatic of Lewis's expository rhetoric and its power are his only two books that directly address particular doctrinal roadblocks. *The Problem of Pain* (1940) and *Miracles: A Preliminary Study* (1947) are both "probabilistic," like most good rhetoric; that is, unlike a logician's or a geometer's proof, or a lawyer's adduction of a "smoking gun," they establish, first possibility, then likelihood. They accomplish this largely by way of "disposition," or structure, and by the appeal of individual arguments. The books are almost devoid of emotional proof.

Lewis's disposition proceeds in these seven stages:

1. frame the problem;

2. define terms;

3. address psychological reservations;

4. address logical objections;

5. hypothesize an explanation for the phenomenon (i.e., the presence of pain in a world created by a loving God, or the apparent defiance of physical laws in the occur-

rence of some concrete, spacio-temporal event—turning water into wine, or raising Lazarus from the dead);

6. demonstrate the greater rationality of the new hypothesis over its competitors; and

7. make the new alternative to disbelief or skepticism
imaginatively and emotionally appealing.

Obviously, refutation (parts 3, 4, and 6) must play a large role
in Lewis's work, as it must in any that attacks a prevalent view,
let alone an entire zeitgeist. Virtually the first half of *Miracles*
is refutative, through the dazzling tenth chapter, "Horrid Red
Things." There, he defines and then rebuts erroneous mental
images evoked by theological or spiritual language. He attempts to demonstrate only the possibility of miracles, not that
any particular one ever occurred, and what they might mean
if they had. The rationale for the possibility makes sense: the
hypothesis coheres.

Often a single paragraph evidences a number of these
functions, accomplishing on the microcosmic scale what the
chapter, or even the whole book, has set out to do. In chapter thirteen of *Miracles*, "On Probability," Lewis establishes
Hume's position (far more clearly than Hume had) that there
is "uniform experience" against miracles. Then this: "Now of
course we must agree with Hume that if there is absolutely
'uniform experience' against miracles, if in other words they
have never happened [which Hume has defined as in fact the
case], why then they never have. Unfortunately we know the
experience against them to be uniform only if we know that
all the reports of them are false. And we can know all the
reports are false only if we know already that miracles have
never occurred. In fact, we are arguing in a circle." Both
Miracles and *The Problem of Pain* follow this seven-function

pattern; most of Lewis's writing contains passages of this kind. He is a difficult author to misunderstand.

The probabilistic goal is also attained by individual argument. We can best approach those arguments in the following terms: Evidence, *therefore* Conclusion, *since* Warrant, *unless* Reservations; or, Socrates is a human being (evidence), *therefore* Socrates is a mortal (conclusion), *since* all men are mortal (warrant), *unless* by "human" we essentially mean an immortal soul made in the image and likeness of God (reservation). Now, rarely in a rhetorical work, as opposed to a strictly logical or philosophical one, will all of these parts be laid out, let alone laid out systematically. Instead, one or more parts are left implicit, sometimes unscrupulously to "avoid the question" of highly dubious assumptions, but usually to save time and the audience's mental energy: They are understood and shared by all, at least in a given audience, so, offers the rhetorician, let us grant them for the sake of the argument.

This mode of rhetorical reasoning is called *enthymemetic* because an argument that suppresses a part is an *enthymeme*. "Socrates is mortal, since all human beings are"—no need to point out that he is one. In *The Problem of Pain*, for example, Lewis assaults a sentimentalized version of a loving God by characterizing it as not reflecting the Father that God actually is but as wish-fulfillment: the sentimentalized version is the *Grand*father everyone would want, he who rampantly indulges his grandchildren, lets them off of every hook, then gives them back, heedless of the formation of their character but satisfied that he is preferred. Lewis assumes we all know, or know of, the feeling, either as grandparents or grandchildren: The assumption warrants his distinction between parent and grandparent and thus his dismissal of the sentimentalized version of God.

In works such as *Miracles* and *The Problem of Pain*, Lewis uses the enthymeme sparingly: its absence is at once what makes those arguments so clear and convincing, on the one hand—exactly like watching a mathematician work out a sum step-by-step so that we come to the conclusion with him— but on the other hand so much more taxing than Lewis's more enthymemetic work, such as *Mere Christianity*, in which the argument is truncated. But whether the work and its arguments be truncated or not, Lewis characteristically refers to his own intellectual difficulties with belief when he was still an atheist; directly addresses his readers, for example, by imputing to them the most rational impatience with what they suppose he is really up to, only to surprise, and thus engage, them by doing the opposite; and uses analogies to press home his point both to the intellect and to the imagination of the audience. Finally, both books, like most of what Lewis wrote, end with perorations of emotional or imaginative moment.

Perhaps Lewis's most remarkable passage is a speech, and a fictional one at that, that best shows his reach. In *The Silver Chair*, a Marsh-Wiggle, one Puddleglum, has accompanied two children on a search for the lost Prince Rilian, who has been held captive by the Queen of Underland. The four are finally free, though still deep in the Queen's cave, when she comes upon them and begins to cast a spell, convincing them that there are no real trees and stars, no Narnia, nor even a real Aslan, the great lion who sang Narnia into creation. At the point of psychological and spiritual collapse, Puddleglum speaks:

> Suppose we have only dreamed, or made up, all those things—trees and grass and sun and moon and stars and Aslan himself. Suppose we have. Then all I can say is that, in that case, the made-up things seem a good deal more

important than the real ones. Suppose this black pit of a kingdom of yours is the only world. Well, it strikes me as a pretty poor one. And that's a funny thing, when you come to think of it. We're just babies making up a game, if you're right. But four babies playing a game can make a play-world which licks your real world hollow. That's why I'm going to stand by the play-world. I'm on Aslan's side even if there isn't any Aslan to lead it. I'm going to live as like a Narnian as I can even if there isn't any Narnia.

Plato's theory of ideas, an ontological proof, the Christian notion of faith, and a defense of legitimate dogma are all in this passage, yet it remains a declaration at once responsive to the situation, appropriate to the speaker, and effective, rousing the others to resistance and freedom.

The rhetorical features of Lewis's microcosmos are unsurprising. He had great dialectical gifts so argument prevails, especially argument by "either-or" disjunctions so well-suited to refutation, in effect Lewis's default mode. He often argues from nature, that is, from human nature and from natural law, and from definition; in these instances, arguments which, if made by others, might be quite drawn out are managed by Lewis with great brevity and ease. But Lewis's ratiocinative gifts are at least matched by his analogical ones, and they enable him to define and communicate extremely demanding concepts with pellucid clarity. I do believe that in examining those gifts, we do not need a microscope so much as an observatory.

Of course he uses these gifts in combination: argument followed by analogy. In fact, the method of argument-and-appeal, though the appeal is by no means always an analogy, is ubiquitous in Lewis's work. Most telling are his uses of the first and second persons, of very plain language, and of frequent reference to familiar circumstances and to himself and his experience. How much more cantankerous, he asks, might the old codger be if he were *not* a Christian, being so naturally cantankerous to begin with? He opens *Mere Christianity* with, "everyone has heard people quarrelling," and within two pages has derived a notion of natural law. Elsewhere, allusions to advertisements and idioms such as "let the cat out of the bag" and "hammer into their heads" abound. He continually refers to his own atheism, will deny direct knowledge of one sin (gambling) while claiming to speak authoritatively of another (lust), and will derogate himself by admitting, for example, that he was wrong about the manageability of the sexual appetite, or by calling himself a prig.

Useful examples of some of these devices, used in combination, occur in a single passage, near the very end of *Miracles*, his longest, most abstract, and nearly his most demanding nonfiction work:

> Perhaps (if I dare to suppose so much) you have been led on at times while you were reading, have felt ancient hopes and fears astir in your heart, have come almost to the threshold of belief—but now? No. It just won't do. Here is the . . . "real" world, round you again. The dream is ending; as all other similar dreams have ended. . . . *Of course* the strange story was false, of course the voice was really subjective. . . . You are ashamed of yourself for having ever thought otherwise: ashamed, relieved, amused, disappointed. . . .

This voice, which is settled yet suggestive, familiar and knowing, almost intimate, yet never hortatory, is ubiquitous in his nonfiction. Oddly, unself-conscious self-characterizations and candid direct address establish a distinctive persona that goes beyond the usual boundaries suggested by the concept of ethical proof. Within the "macrocosmic" region, a number of rhetorical patterns are surprising, and most derive from one startling fact: Never does Lewis attempt directly to confirm— to establish the truth of with certainty—any Christian doctrine or dogma. As he would say, the reader continues to say "I believe" rather than "*eureka!*" His method is *maieutic*: In his understanding of his audience's expectations (which for the purpose of an engaging surprise he may deliberately violate) and of their semantic and intellectual conventions, he helps give birth to their gestating belief. He is precisely the midwife described by Debra Winger.

IV

Lewis knows his audience and their setting well enough to reduce the risks of his midwifery. He sometimes calls direct attention to the fundamental biases of the ordinary reader, diagnoses their linguistic shortcomings, and suggests lines of argument that have had an impact, in his own experience, on general audiences. In *God in the Dock*, he points out to clergymen that, "A century ago our task was to edify those who had been brought up in the Faith: our present task is chiefly to convert and instruct infidels; Great Britain is as much a part of the mission field as China." He insists that the problem is often one of "translation." To the 1945 assembly of Anglican priests and youth leaders he first described his audience's historical and textual skepticism and their general lack of a sense of sin; then he listed eighteen concepts about which there is either a deep misunderstanding or total ignorance. Among these are atonement (erroneously taken to mean mere compensation), charity (as alms), Christian (as "a decent chap"),

creative (as talented), dogma (as "unproved assertion delivered in an arrogant manner"), personal (as corporeal), and
spiritual (as "immaterial" and always good: "They don't really
believe that envy could be as bad as drunkenness.").

Every examination for ordinands, he insists, ought to include a passage from some standard theological work for translation into the vernacular. Among our contemporary biases
is the tendency to reverse the ancient attitude and to approach
God as the accused; "if God should have a reasonable defense
. . . the trial may even end in God's acquittal. But the important thing is that Man is on the Bench and God is in the Dock."
Thus must an apologist insist that "Christianity is a statement
which, if false, is of no importance, and, if true, of infinite
importance." This cannot be accomplished by patronizing the
audience, for "uneducated people are not irrational people. .
. . Often, indeed, the novelty of [sustained argument]. . . de-
lights them."

Here is a perfect (I choose the word advisedly) example.
"Meditation in a Toolshed," a twelve-hundred-word essay which
appeared originally in *The Coventry Evening Telegraph* (July
17, 1945), shows us Lewis's gifts unadorned; there is no exalted
peroration or promise of glory, but it alters the terms of the
debate and is among the best things Lewis ever wrote—and
for a most modest audience of perhaps uneducated, but certainly not irrational, readers:

> I was standing today in the dark toolshed. The sun was
> shining outside and through the crack at the top of the
> door there came a sunbeam. From where I stood that
> beam of light, with the specks of dust floating in it, was
> the most striking thing in the place. Everything else was
> almost pitch-black. I was seeing the beam, not seeing
> things by it. Then I moved so that the beam fell on my

eyes. Instantly the whole previous picture vanished. I saw no toolshed, and (above all) no beam. Instead I saw, framed in the irregular cranny at the top of the door, green leaves moving on the branches of a tree outside and beyond that, 90 odd million miles away, the sun. Looking along the beam, and looking at the beam are very different experiences. . . . The savage dances in ecstasy at midnight before Nyonga and feels with every muscle that his dance is helping to bring the new green crops and the spring rain and the babies. The anthropologist, observing that savage, records that he is performing a fertility ritual of the type so-and-so. . . . You get one experience of a thing when you look along it and another when you look at it. Which is the "true" or "valid" experience? Which tells you most about the thing? And you can hardly ask that question without noticing that for the last fifty years or so everyone has been taking the answer for granted. The people who look *at* things have had it all their own way; the people who look *along* things have simply been brow-beaten. It has even come to be taken for granted that the external account of a thing somehow refutes or "debunks" the account given from inside. "All these moral ideals which look so transcendental and beautiful from inside," says the wiseacre, "are really only a mass of biological instincts and inherited taboos." And no one plays the game the other way round by replying, "If only you will step inside, the things that look to you like instincts and taboos will suddenly reveal their real and transcendental nature." That, in fact, is the whole basis of the specifically "modern" type of thought. I might have discounted what I saw when looking along the beam (i.e., the leaves moving and the sun) on the ground that it was "really only a strip of dusty light in a dark shed". But then that side vision is itself an instance of the activity we call seeing. And this new instance could also be looked at from the outside. I could allow a scientist to tell me that what seemed to be a beam of light in a shed was "really only an agitation of my own optic nerves". And that would be just as good (or as bad) a bit of debunking as the previous one. In other words, you can step outside one experience only by stepping inside another. Therefore, if all inside experiences are always misleading, we are always misled.

We see here many features typical of Lewis: the philosophy made comprehensible, of course, but also the analogical gift, the popular tone, the militant stance against modern thought, the analytical sharpness, the re-establishment of an intellectual ground for the sort of response (and argument based upon it) of which the ordinary person has been made to feel ashamed, and the absence of argument on behalf of any specifically Christian doctrine. Lewis unbegs the question, so to speak, by revealing the modern assumption to be as much a dogma as any traditional one; and it is much simpler to read than Alexander's *Space, Time and Deity*. Such an analytical passage contrasts with others not quite so plain. When Lewis needs to depict, rather than to explain, man's destiny, he often invokes some variation of *Sehnsucht*, which frequently gives rise to the images of hope and glory that form so many of Lewis's appeals, especially in his perorations and throughout the fictions.

These images "make" the reader, not by imposing, but by occasioning, belief. In *Letters to Malcolm*, Lewis makes this point in a discussion of "servile fear," which he calls "the lowest form of religion," since no believable God would be entirely safe or "tame"; even though the old divines "exhausted their eloquence in arousing such fear," they had to admit it did not last more than a few hours after the sermon. And then he notes that "the soul that has once been waked, or stung, or uplifted, by the desire of God, will inevitably (I think) awake to the fear of losing him." Notwithstanding his concrete depictions of evil, Lewis never uses bald fear of the sort resembling the motivating horror of, say, that old divine Jonathan Edwards in his justly famed and enormously effective sermon "Sinners in the Hands of an Angry God":

> There is nothing that keeps wicked men at any one moment out of hell but the mere pleasure of God. . . . Yea, God is a great deal more angry with great numbers that are now on earth, yea, doubtless, with many that are now in this congregation, that it may be, are at ease and quiet, than he is with many of those that are now in the flames of hell. The creation groans with you; the creature is made subject to the bondage of your corruption. . . . The bow of God's wrath is bent, and the arrow made ready on the string . . . and it is nothing but the mere pleasure of God that . . . keeps the arrow one moment from being made drunk with your blood. . . . Yea, there is nothing else that is to be given as a reason why you don't this very moment drop down into hell . . . he will crush you under his feet without mercy; he'll crush out your blood and make it fly. . . . He will not only hate you but have you in the utmost contempt.

Instead, Lewis tells us that "all the leaves of the New Testament are rustling with the rumor" that we will not always be on the wrong side of the door. Some day, God willing, we shall get in. And we are not ordinary: "You have never talked to a mere mortal. Nations, cultures, arts, civilizations—these are mortal, and their life is to ours as the life of a gnat." Elsewhere he amplifies: "Someday we may ride bareback, confident and rejoicing, those greater mounts, those winged and world-shaking horses which perhaps even now expect us with impatience." The final page of Lewis's final book, *Letters to Malcolm*, contains a typically inviting image of hope, his last effort at midwifery: "Then the new earth and sky, the same yet not the same as these, will rise in us as we have risen in Christ. And once again, after who knows what aeons of silence and the dark, the birds will sing and the waters flow, and lights and shadows move across the hill, and the faces of our friends laugh upon us with amazed recognition. Guesses . . . only guesses . . . ." In the last peroration he ever wrote the images of hope and of mercy beckon demonstratively, "putting it," as Aristotle said, "before their eyes."

Lewis's style was well-adjusted to its audience and purpose, perhaps perfectly so, removed from the colloquial, not decorated, often rendered in quite idiomatic English. He can write passages of great height, but largely allows his thought to accumulate slowly; his often mischievous humor is always part of the argumentative context, usually on behalf of moderation in controversy. His language discriminates sharply, and his clarity is therefore severe: no "caring, sharing, and daring." His humor derives from his analogies, but they incarnate the thought; so humor—or wit—seems to become thought itself. Our attitude towards the subject matter might very well be serious but not necessarily grave. Lest the reader be inattentive, he is addressed, directly: Lewis's language is the reader's own; his examples, ordinary and recognizable; his cadence, that of familiar speed. He anticipates objections as though he has read the reader's mind when, in fact, he has read his own experience and that told him by others, and then thought it out to "the *ruddy* end." Within that voice there is a concrete and particular person, and it will address only other concrete and particular persons—into which the reader, to his delighted surprise, is made for the duration. A common ground is held against a common foe.

While addressing members of the Electric and Musical Industries Union, for example, Lewis answered a question about the outward signs of Christian surrender with a common touch designed to establish just such a common ground with his audience: "I think of the advertisements for 'White Smiles' Tooth Paste, saying that it is the best on the market." He proceeds to distinguish between those possessed of naturally healthy teeth and those who are not and use the toothpaste. And always there are analogies: faith is like the feeling we have when entering a very familiar, but momentarily darkened, room; Christ is like the experienced mountain-climber in whom the inexperienced must trust—personally— if he is to get across a chasm; the Trinity is like a cube, or books resting upon a table, or a bulb and the light it emits.

Sometimes one can over-analyze, especially a writer's use of a plain style. I recall being particularly impressed by Lewis's use of a single word—"fix"—in *The Screwtape Letters*, when uncle Screwtape advises Wormwood to "fix [the patient's] attention" on his own feelings, as though their presence or absence were the heart of religious belief. The word was forceful: brief, sharp, and suggestive, not only of attachment but of a proper and permanent putting into place, as with a very strong glue. I did not suppose that Lewis had labored over the word, but any lack of labor did not diminish its felicity; labor or not, its use remained a conscious rhetorical choice of considerable artistry. Or so I thought until I studied the *Screwtape* manuscript. There I saw that Lewis had written "rivit," then (intuiting that he had misspelled the word) "revit," and next "rivet"; but by then his confidence was overly-taxed and, not knowing that he had spelled the word correctly, again struck out the attempt and in a larger, bolder hand than he had used wrote "FIX."

Humility and companionability, stylistic ease and metaphysical depth, and a regard for the reader all combine to make the thought sensible and pleasing, another violation of an expectation encouraged by most theological writing. Lewis warned other apologists that highly popular writing, because simple, is much longer than more technical writing; but he must have meant longer to write. Neither natural conversation nor its extension is longer to read, hear, or understand.

6

Rhetorica Religii

Lewis, not Richard Baxter, might have written what follows, from chapter nincteen, "An Exercise of this Heavenly Contemplation for the Help of the Unskilful," in
The Saint's Everlasting Rest: "How long shall I see the Church
of Christ be trodden under the feet of persecutors . . . ? Alas
that I must stand by and see the Church and cause of Christ,
like a football in the midst of a crowd of boys, tossed about
in contention from one to another; everyone running, and
sweating with foolish violence, and labouring the downfall of
all that are in his way, and all to get it into his own power. . .
till they have driven it on to the goal of their private interests
of deluded fancies! There is none of this disorder in the heavenly Jerusalem. . . ."

I

The characteristic *topoi*, and the relationship among them, that
bring order to Lewis's rhetorical world are not necessarily
coordinate with each other. Some speak to the nature of man

(i.e., Lewis's "anthropology," as in "Man is a machine meant to run on God"), some to his psychology, others to relationships between people, and still others to a supernature and its relationship to us. Their functions vary as well. Sometimes they permute other ideas, sometimes they stand alone; and at still other times they are unspoken assumption. Often they are distinctions, which Lewis makes so adroitly: between looking *at* and *along*, for example, or between excusing and forgiving; between *wondelone* and *hluntheline* (a too-little noticed distinction between two kinds of longing, from Lewis's invented Old Solar language introduced in *Out of the Silent Planet*), or Faith-A and Faith-B. Sometimes these distinctions take the form of disjunctions: Either Jesus was a lunatic along the lines of a man who thinks himself "a poached egg," or he was who he claims to be; either you tell God, "Thy will be done," or he will tell you.

Collectively the *topoi* describe, or evoke, or awaken us to the otherness towards which we would regress or to obstacles in our path. It is unfortunate that there is no one book called *Lewis's Topics*, although there are several good ones on different aspects of his thinking (e.g., Gilbert Meilaender's *The Taste for the Other*, William Luther White's *The Image of Man in C. S. Lewis*, Richard L. Purtill's *C. S. Lewis's Case for Christianity*, and Michael D. Aeschliman's *The Restitution of Man: C. S. Lewis and the Case Against Scientism*), and Hooper includes a "Key Ideas" section in his *Companion & Guide*. What follows excludes ideas that are either strictly political (about democracy, for example) or theological (with one exception):

1. Joy (or *Sehnsucht*), especially as a rationale for heaven;

2. the validity (not the happiest choice of words, as we shall see later on) of reason, that is, reason as a participation

in the divine Logos: You cannot cut out "the organ" and still "demand the function";

3. the objectivity of the natural law, which Lewis calls the Tao in *The Abolition of Man*;

4. the epistemological reliability of the imagination, especially when realized in the forms of metaphor, symbolism, and myth, to establish meaning, the antecedent of truth;

5. the solidity of the supernatural world and its imminence;

6. the Law of Inattention, which enjoins us to appreciate

7. the quiddity of things and of looking away from the self; like other ages we have our cultural myths which militate against religious belief; to embrace these myths while patronizing previous ages is

8. chronological snobbery, "the uncritical acceptance of the intellectual climate common to our own age and the assumption that whatever has gone out of date is on that account discredited. You must find out why it went out of date. Was it ever refuted . . or did it merely die away as fashions do?";

9. authority, hierarchy, and ceremony are prominent features of the supernatural landscape;

10. membership, in the Body of Christ, not as sub-individual units of a mass but as differentiated "organs," the Persons we were always meant to be;

11. transposition, the idea that this world has fewer musical notes, so to speak, than the next and so must "double up" on its keys (as in erotic imagery symbolizing religious devotion) in order to communicate the next world in this —a vindication of

12. sacramentalism, the idea that the next world is not merely imminent but present, if only we

13. pay attention to the Signs;

14. we do that by looking both At and Along, that is, by both Contemplation and Enjoyment;

15. obedience is our main job: we were "born to obey" and have no "right to happiness";

16. "Bulverism," the insistence that an argument is not refuted simply by virtue of attributing motive to the person who has made it;

17. the Law of Undulation, which reminds us that states of feeling come and go and are not the essence of religious devotion or—especially—of love, which, as Madeleine L'Engle reminds us in *A Wind in the Door*, is not something you feel but something you do: "Feelings come and go," Lewis wrote, "but mostly they go";

18. the Inner Ring Syndrome, the temptation to compromise ourselves, from small things like joke-telling and gossip to big things like political corruption, in order to be accepted by power-brokers;

19. ordinateness is the suitable, that is, the ordained or natural matching of response to stimulus, as in a literary stock response which finds virtue lovely;

20. first and second things reminds us of the need for perspective and context: A pleasure, for example, or a real good, must not be elevated above its station, because not only will other pleasures and goods be sacrificed but the original will be diminished;

21. personhood is not personality, rather, "it is the instrument through which you see God," not unlike a lens;

22. progress is not necessarily moving forward in the direction you happen to be facing, as we have come to believe, but movement towards the right goal—which may lie in a different direction; and

23. verbicide, the killing of words by inflation, imprecision, or equivocal use for partisan purpose, slays thought when not merely distorting it. We must combat verbicide at least by not committing it ourselves for, as Lewis put it in one of his many and ample annotations to his copy of I. A. Richards's *Practical Criticism*, "Words are the meeting points at which regions of experience which can never combine . . . come together. They are the occasions and means of that growth which is the mind's endless endeavor to order itself. . . . It is no mere signalling system."

The salient feature, at once revealing and fundamental, shared by these ideas is the quality, except for number ten, of not being particularly Christian, nor in most cases even religious. They are of the first order of importance because they inform Lewis's entire world of discourse and because he writes of them explicitly, recommending them to us as interpretive instruments and as axioms to be proceeded *from*. They name, inflect, and qualify experience. If beliefs and doctrines of faith and of morals are Lewis's vocabulary, then these are his "syntax." By way of them Lewis retrieved the muscle, bone, and sinew of a singular, coherent belief: its reasonableness—without which the returns of exhortation constantly diminish, and with which it becomes virtually unnecessary. The ironic playing out of this *faculty of permutation* within Lewis's internal and poetic landscapes was wonderfully suited to his formidably militant intellect, turning it into a tensile and glittering vehicle of Christian belief.

But sometimes Lewis misfires. If there is anything I wish

he had not written it is "Delinquents in the Snow," a fairly late essay, splenetic nearly to the point of tantrum; pardonable, I think, as it was provoked by the disturbance of the pain-ridden Joy, who was finally getting some sleep until the disturbance. That is a tonal impropriety. A substantive flaw occurs in Book I, chapter 2 of *Mere Christianity*, "The Invasion." Lewis is entertaining the question of whether goodness is so because God ordains it, or good *per se*. Could God make badness good? The question is further complicated by the introduction of Dualism: What would be the fate of the natural law if two equal but opposite gods existed? Lewis's answer is that "badness is only spoiled goodness." To play fair Lewis posits a morally neutral universe. Then, in describing the bad power, Lewis writes, "To be bad, he must exist and have intelligence and will. But existence, intelligence, and will are in themselves good." But why? Unless Lewis is "arguing in circles" by sneaking the law into his morally neutral hypothesis, there is no grounds on which to call *anything* good.

The most famous example of Lewisian logical difficulty involves Elizabeth Anscombe, the philosophy tutor at Somerville College who at the Socratic Club in February of 1948 responded to Lewis's thesis that naturalism is self-refuting. He had argued that the independent faculty of reason is "invalid" if it is natural, atoms randomly bumping into other atoms like the rest of creation (according to the Materialists). How can I trust a conclusion if it was pre-determined by anything, including randomly moving atoms? Anscombe attacked Lewis's use of "valid," pointing out that its application in this case was technically flawed: Why something is true is not the same as why I should think it so. Anscombe's argument is beautifully elaborated and sufficiently probative to have caused Lewis to revise the chapter, making it considerably

longer than it had been. Some say that Lewis spoke of the
encounter with great distress, wondering why Anscombe, a
Catholic, had not at least offered an alternative; but Anscombe
herself heard from spectators who knew Lewis well that that
was not the case. She recalls it as a "sober discussion of certain quite definite criticisms" and characterizes the descriptions of Lewis's distress by others as "an interesting example
of the phenomenon called 'projection'."

I think Anscombe was right, though somewhat less so than
she believes. Her argument is too subtle and long to bear
analysis here, but I do believe she errs in failing to discuss an
argument as a "psychological event," which is, after all, Lewis's
main point, and that she shifts from "reason"—a formally valid,
self-contained argument—to "cause"—the ultimate explanation, not of a particular conclusion, but of our ability to make
arguments, to see the world ordinately at all: *Logos.* One's very
ability to discern formal validity presupposes an independence
in that process of discernment; or, as Lewis might put it, to
examine reason one cannot step outside the beam of reasoning except into another beam of reasoning. No matter how
hard we try, we must look *along*, not *at*. (Lewis's annotations
make clear that as far back as his first encounter with Joseph's
An Introduction to Logic he was grappling with the question,
What happens to reasoning when one attempts to examine *it*?)

The other attack upon Lewis's work that merits consideration is John Beversluis's *C. S. Lewis and the Search for Rational Religion* (1985). Beversluis sometimes seems to agree
with William Butler Yeats's snide "What is rhetoric but the will
trying to do the work of the imagination?" Beversluis is a
trained philosopher who makes no *ad hominem* attacks and
is generous in his praise of an opponent's achievements; and
along the way he does call attention to logically weak links

of the kind I think I have found in *Mere Christianity* and described above. But his case is badly overextended and based, ultimately, on a series of strawmen both large and small. Among the latter is his faulting Lewis for not building a case for Christianity on "rock-hard evidence," as Lewis claimed he would; of course, Lewis never did make such a claim. Among the former is an insistence upon the literal, verbatim facticity of *A Grief Observed*, which is not only naive but contradictory, since Beversluis faults Lewis for lacking an existential faith that Lewis in fact recovers in that very book. Would that Beversluis had read Otto, let alone read him with Lewis's attentiveness, for then he, too, would have known what Lewis learned early: The Holy, as opposed to the *idea* of the Holy, cannot be rationally sought after.

What gives away Beversluis's game, I believe, is his too-great reliance on one essay by Lewis, "Obstinacy in Belief." That reliance betrays Beversluis's profound ignorance of the demands of rhetoric: He is generically tone-deaf, rather like a man who knows the words to a song but not its music and yet goes on anyway as though he were singing. Admittedly, there is good precedence for Beversluis; for example, the Socrates of Plato's *Gorgias*. I wish, however, that Beversluis had gone on, as Richard Weaver did, to a serious consideration of Plato's *Phaedrus*, wherein the philosopher-dialectician not only admits a place for rhetoric but practices it at its most sublime. Then he might have understood Lewis's method without having underestimated his intellectual independence and the wholeness of his achievement.

Edmund Crispin's professor-detective, Gervase Fenn, once remarked, "I always think psychology is wrong in imagining that when it has analyzed evil it has somehow disposed of it." Beversluis might make such a mistake, but Lewis could not, which is why his *topoi* remain so pertinent. Over twenty years ago Christopher Lasch diagnosed and condemned the "culture of narcissism"; at about the same time Paul Vitz wrote *Psychology as Religion: The Cult of Self-Worship*, a book praised by no less a medical man than Karl Menninger, who himself wrote—that he might have read Lewis's advice to Anglican priests and youth leaders is easy to imagine—*Whatever Became of Sin?* More recently Richard Webster has written *Why Freud Was Wrong: Sin, Science and Psychoanalysis* (1995), in which he expands upon Lewis's notion that Freud would have been quite fine if he had limited himself to science, instead of working out his own religious and messianic impulses *as though* they were science. Further vindication of Lewis's thought (though given his view of "originality" Lewis would disavow that attribution) comes from James Q. Wilson's *The Moral Sense* (1993) and Alasdair MacIntyre's influential *After Virtue* (1981). Both men either assume, argue for, or conclude what Lewis had so cogently and alarmingly pressed upon us fifty years ago: that the natural law exists and reason is the instrument whereby we discern it. Wilson could easily have had Chapter 1 of *The Abolition of Man* in mind for his discussion of training; and he ends his book with a virtual echo of Lewis's *dictum* that we cannot amputate the organ and still demand its function.

Lewis's reasonableness and coherence; his varied and cogent structure of argument-and-appeal; his enthymemetic invitation to participation by the reader; his surprising reversals, Chestertonian inversions, and useful distinctions; his reliable and consistent "syntax" of *topoi*, analogical familiarity, beckoning images of glory; and his avoidance of anything remotely hortatory—together these features of Lewis's rhetorical landscape make it at least inviting, often compelling. As appealing as the landscape is, there is more: In either merely visiting or deciding to dwell therein we hear Lewis's *voice*, which is more than the sum total of stylistic devices and difficult to analyze at all. "Literary criticism in medieval England," he wrote in a book review, "is a subject which would seem at first sight to admit the same terse treatment as the snakes of Iceland"—no, not "Ireland," "*Iceland*." That sentence has a signature. A young boy wrote to him proclaiming how wonderful it was that God had made dogs for us; "How do you know," Lewis wrote back, "that God didn't make us for dogs?" One can almost "feel the air move," as actors say of a good performance. That he may have meant that more literally than we at first suspect is not beside the point. In *Surprised by Joy* he remarks on his old dog Tim:

> By now he and I were less like master and dog than like two friendly visitors in the same hotel. We met constantly, passed the time of day, and parted with much esteem to follow our own paths. I think he had one friend of his own species, a neighboring red setter; a very respectable, middle-aged dog. Perhaps a good influence; for poor Tim, though I loved him, was the most undisciplined, unaccomplished, and dissipated-looking creature that ever went on four legs. He never exactly obeyed you; he sometimes agreed with you.

—a movement of the air that, as Peter Kreeft has put it in quite another context, turns space into place. There could hardly be more intelligence, virtue, and good will, let alone charm and surprise, than we meet in that paragraph. And intelligence, virtue, and good will are the essences, according to Aristotle, of "personal proof"; in this case, better called *presence*, that extension of natural conversation, as though at the same time,

in the same place, face-to-face with the reader—abundant,
attentive, knowing, and charitable.

II

Withal he was as troubled by his own devices as he was impatient with the art behind them. By now we cannot be surprised that in his notebooks he will casually use "rhetoric" and
"rhetorical" as derogatory terms. Of his narrative poem *The
Queen of Drum* he wrote, "the old [attempt at] smelting down
a nasty bit of factual stuff into poetry. . . only succeeds in
expanding it into rhetoric." When he treats of the *Anti-
claudianus* of Alanus de Insulis in a draft of his section on
rhetoric for *The Discarded Image,* he cannot help ending with
the single judgment, "abominably rhetorical." More telling are
the instances when he brings his own fictional rhetoric to a
halt. During the debate on Perelandra, the wrong side has the
better rhetoric; Ransom "won" only because he acts, non-rhe-
torically, by punching the Un-man in his mouth. The only
passenger on the *Great Divorce* bus to Heaven who stays is the
one who stops rhetorizing and exclaims, "Damn and blast you!
Go on can't you? Get it over," and presently shuts up. At the
end of *Till We Have Faces,* the queen writes of what had been
her lucid and rather convincing complaint, "Only words, words;
to be led out to battle with other words." And in *The Silver
Chair* Puddleglum's affirmation follows his determining action:
With his naked webbed-foot he stamps on the fire that is
complicit in the witch's verbal spell. The rhetorical genius in
Lewis governed uneasily.

Some who knew him saw a certain mystery about him, not
secretiveness or a mere preference for privacy, but actual
mystery. And we might ask—about a man with so strong a

potential light of his own, so fierce a will to bring it into brightness, and so clear a lens as his had surely become—how *not*
a mystery? His old, ambivalent view of rhetoric is intimately
tied to his equally ambivalent view of one's self and the Christian demand that it be transcended. What he finds discom-
forting—even alarming—is its hold upon him, and that this
hold symptomizes an inability to let go of his old, needful, theatrical ego. In the private venue of lyric poetry, unpublished
during his lifetime, this alarm surfaces explicitly in "As the Ruin
Falls," addressed perhaps to Joy Davidman, perhaps to God:

> *All this is flashy rhetoric about loving you.*
> *I never had a selfless thought since I was born.*
> *I am mercenary and self-seeking through and through:*
> *I want God, you, all friends, merely to serve my turn.*

> *Peace, re-assurance, pleasure, are the goals I seek*
> *I cannot crawl one inch outside my proper skin:*
> *I talk of love—a scholar's parrot may talk Greek—*
> *But, self-imprisoned, always end where I begin.*

And therein lies the problem. The self upon which Lewis's
genius of the will turned its back is the very same self so pal-
pably conspiring with his genius of rhetoric, the very same
rhetoric that issued forth in response to his willed commitment to a vocation, that same self that John Wain told us so
enjoyed an audience and which Lewis—"coyly," I have said—
warned us against discussing. In his chapter on pride in *Mere
Christianity,* "The Great Sin," he tells us that God is trying to
make us humble for our own sake, "trying to take off a lot of
silly, ugly, fancy-dress" of self-conceit that we are wearing. And
then he confesses, "I wish I had got a bit further with humility myself: if I had, I could probably tell you more about the
relief, the comfort, of taking the fancy-dress off—getting rid
of the false self, with all its 'Look at me . . .'."

In yet another poem not published during his lifetime, "The Apologist's Evening Prayer," the dilemma of self-denial versus self-exploitation brought him virtually to the brink of despair:

> *From all my lame defeats and oh! much more*
> *From all the victories that I seemed to score;*
> *From cleverness shot forth on Thy behalf*
> *At which, while angels weep, the audience laugh;*
> *From all my proofs of Thy divinity,*
> *Thou, who wouldst give no sign, deliver me.*
>
> *Thoughts are but coins. Let me not trust, instead*
> *Of Thee, their thin-worn image of Thy head.*
> *From all my thoughts, even from my thoughts of Thee,*
> *O thou fair Silence, fall, and set me free.*
> *Lord of the narrow gate and needle's eye,*
> *Take from me all my trumpery lest I die.*

In Christian terms the spiritual dilemma is clear. When rhetoric and redemption meet in the self, one of them must give way, since rhetoric requires a voluble ego and redemption its death an antecedent to its rebirth and resurrection. Almost twenty-five years ago Owen Barfield wrote to me that he did not think Lewis's persona—the "pastiche" over which Barfield had proclaimed—was deliberately adopted. "The indifference to self" that came later, continued Barfield, "may well have been responsible for his *maintaining* the persona throughout the rest of his life, as may also have been the thought of its usefulness for the purpose of argumentative Christian apology." Here is the crux of the matter: Will has directed a vocation that requires self-exhibition, with the object of that vocation being self-denial. Spirit understands the latter but enjoys the former. And since neither reason nor imagination offers any way out, Lewis despairs. Is there a paradigm, adaptable to rhetorical

theory, that can lift both Lewis and the critic out of the quan-
dary? One that might describe Lewis's method without forc-
ing or overlooking the biographical and rhetorical facts?

Ordinarily we would classify Lewis's books into the categories of fiction, apologetics, scholarship, and poetry, with
the further refinement of "short" and "long" introduced into
each category. Thus *The Chronicles of Narnia* would be in the
same class as *Till We Have Faces*; *The Pilgrim's Regress* and *Out
of the Silent Planet* would be in the same class; and so would
Letters to an American Lady and Lewis's letters to Arthur
Greeves. We could add distinctions and slice into the work
more deeply still. For example, we could distinguish formally
between essays, sermons, and other addresses; or between
children's fiction and fiction for adults. These categories tell
us something about the correspondence between rhetorical
purpose and rhetorical strategy; but they do not tell us enough,
and the "miscellaneous" category would be uselessly large.
Finally, we could neaten things up by noting when, or at which
stage, a certain work was written. The result would be a sort
of three-dimensional grid, with the three axes corresponding
to type (very refined), reach (not length), and period of the
work. This appears impressive, but it turns out to be usefully
descriptive, yet otherwise unavailing. To achieve something
more explanatory than descriptive we would need an odd taxonomy, one that would enable us to apprehend, not C. S. Lewis
as a theologian, a philosopher, or even a literary practitioner,
but Lewis as he was essentially: the wary yet energetic, ambivalent yet committed *Homo rhetoricus*.

One category might be named "Personal," to indicate in
which of his capacities Lewis is writing; another "At," a third
"Along"; then "Voice," indicating Lewis's tone and thus his
intended audience; a fifth for "Content," and a sixth for "Au-

tobiography." The problem is one of any taxonomy: rampant overlapping. In Lewis's case the problem is aggravated by the need for a seventh category. After all, any student of Lewis's does not need an elaborate apparatus to know that rhetorically things changed in the very late 1940s and for a dozen or so years thereafter. Certain delays brought on by Flora's death were coming to an end, and the genius of the will was redirecting the great engine, though not without some considerable, one might say, sputtering. If he had declared it publicly we must indeed call it angst; but he did not, so I will not. There is considerable difference between the self used as a *datum* and posturing, of which Lewis was simply incapable.

The public change is this: *Lewis began to put even his rhetorical self aside.* Thus that seventh category: not merely "Oblique" to designate all his fictions, but a sub-category therein that can only and best be called "Feigned" or, better, "Veiled." There are exceptions in the *period*, of course—collections of sermons and essays, *The Four Loves*, additional literary scholarship and history—and the category is not without precedent prior to this period—Barfield's cry of *"pastiche!"* with respect to *The Personal Heresy* of the mid-1930s mark it as a muted, but revealing, antecedent, as is *The Pilgrim's Regress*, though it is hardly veiled since, as allegory, the "feigning" is candid. The "veiled" books I am referring to are *The Magician's Nephew* (1955), *Surprised by Joy* (1955), *Till We Have Faces* (1956), *Reflections on the Psalms* (1958), *A Grief Observed* (1961), and *Letters to Malcolm: Chiefly on Prayer* (1964).

Surprised by Joy has already been discussed, for what it both conceals and distorts, my point having been the existence of at least two worlds: the Official, with one version for Albert and another for Minto, and the Deeper, the existence of which calls into question the accuracy of Lewis's diagno-

sis, though not the sincerity of his conscious claim, of atheism—at least these two worlds in addition to his Inner and
Outer. *Reflections on the Psalms* denies intentions that are
nevertheless fulfilled. Lewis writes, "I am 'comparing notes',
not presuming to instruct"; and later he continues: "Finally,
as will soon be apparent to any reader, this is not what is called
an apologetic work. I am nowhere trying to convince unbe-
lievers that Christianity is true. I address those who already
believe it, or those who are ready, while reading, to 'suspend
their disbelief'. A man can't be always defending the truth;
there must be a time to feed on it." Now, the very presence of
a disclaimer is among the oldest tricks in the proverbial book:
"I come not . . . to steal away your hearts," says Mark Antony,
"I am no orator as Brutus is. . . ." Perhaps Lewis was trying
to convince himself. In the event, there is some moralizing
and much argument in the book: The rhetorical effect—an
apologetic effect—is among those produced.

Letters to Malcolm is feigned, too, in the same disarming
way as, but far more thoroughly than, *Reflections on the Psalms*.
"Thank Betty for her note. I'll come by the later train, the 3:40."
But there is no Betty and there is no Malcolm. Believing otherwise, however, makes a subtle but important difference to
the reader, who thought he was catching a real epistolist un-
awares. To be sure, the convention is an old one, but not to
us, trained by "the media," as we are, to be literal-minded.
These letters are more artful than any he wrote to genuine
intimates, since he intends, as private letters do not, a "third
party" to "contemplate" his quite unsystematic meditation. On
the other hand, they let much more self out of the bag than
he ever did to a stranger with whom he happened to corre-
spond, such as "The American Lady," a posthumous book
edited by Clyde Kilby. The rhetorical formula has no mys-

tery: the more casual, informal, and intimate the discourse, the less contrived and therefore believable. Lewis's impatience with the many readers who were disappointed to learn that the letters are not real as such has always struck me as a bit petulant, if not disingenuous. In any event, all three books are avowedly by C. S. Lewis and, although they somehow distort or seek to disarm, present a version true to various aspects of this complex self. That is not the case with the other three books.

Thematically *Till We Have Faces* is Lewis from beginning to end. The god and his castle, for example, are concrete, though intangible and invisible to Orual; in fact more real than Orual, who comes to realize that she was but a shadow compared to them. Can the peroration of *Miracles* not be called to mind? Or the denouement of *The Last Battle*? Or the premise of *The Great Divorce*, wherein the heavenly rain is so real it drills through the ectoplasmic bodies of the visiting Shades? We have been prepared for Orual's possessiveness by *The Four Loves* and *The Great Divorce*, where we are shown a woman like Orual and are told that Hell should not be allowed to blackmail Heaven. And Psyche, who always longed to live on the mountain as though it were her real home, is she not like the regressing John the Pilgrim? Is she not also surprised by Joy? Many other distinctly Lewisian themes abound; but three, which are evident in much of his thought, I believe to be at the center of meaning in *Till We Have Faces*. Grace, the unmerited gift that transcends argument, could account for the "improbability" of the change in Orual in Part ii; Membership, the purposeful functioning of a part within the Mysterious Body, allows for the interchange of labors; and the Law of Inattention, which Orual violates wholesale.

Whereas Lewis's usual technique is to mythologize (or to

re-mythologize), in *Till We Have Faces* he is "de-mythologiz-ing," painting an intimate portrait of a brilliant, willful, and resentful mind who is angry with the gods for not existing, to paraphrase Lewis about himself. Glome is not another world and does not exist in another dimension; we do not discover—as we do in *Perelandra* or in the short story "Forms of Things Unknown"—that the myth is historically accurate. We remain on Earth, and we are shown that the myth is historically false. The most important of all differences, though, is that of nar-rative perspective, which is unlike any we are accustomed to in Lewis. Doubtless, we have seen the first person elsewhere (*Perelandra, The Great Divorce*), but that is always "Lewis"; here, the first person is a stranger, and a woman, and a not-very-likable woman—self-serving, belligerent, and filled with mili-tantly anti-divine delusions. She is uncharacteristically ugly and ambivalent, too. The exclusion of traditional elements and the inclusion of a strikingly new one should serve to forewarn us. Orual, or the self she is projecting like the Tragedian on the fringe of Heaven, is not quite who she seems to be, least of all to herself. In the end it is Orual who will be found out.

Till We Have Faces is an example of a book to which, given its relative unpopularity, even presumably informed readers are insufficiently submissive. But why should that surprise us? I believe Lewis himself was wrong in saying that it is about a woman corrupted by possessive love. That may be what he intended, but he produced very much more. There is noth-ing false in this tale. If read correctly it can enlarge any reader—especially a post-modern one. It requires no Chris-tian belief and addresses a question which nearly monopo-lizes the contemporary mind: What is Personhood and what are we to make of it? The book gives an answer, as does much of Lewis's work. It is so basic that it underlies the rest of the entire syntax of Lewis's thought. It is, to paraphrase him, what the story is about, his version of a person in despair, not knowing it, but on the brink and finally being brought over, "kicking and screaming." She has projected an Open self, nurtured a Hidden self (she spends virtually all of her adulthood behind a veil), avoided her Blind self, and denied her Unknown self, her version of Lewis's Deeper life. It is Orual's own *Surprised by Joy*, with both books ending in exactly the same place—their narrators having taken the leap of faith. I have often thought that if Orual had not died she would have kept on writing, eventually rendering her version of "As the Ruin Falls." Lewis of course did. In the end it is Orual, and Lewis, and we who will be found out, for Orual is a surrogate for us all in this, his fourth "autobiography."

But this a modest contrivance compared with one of Lewis's last books. He published it pseudonymously, and it is his shortest book. In 1940 he had given us *The Problem of Pain*, a "contemplation"; in 1961 there appeared *A Grief Observed*. It purports to be the diary he kept immediately upon the death of his wife and thus an "enjoyment" of pain. The former is a telling, the latter, a showing. How would this great Christian, this pontificating "chap," this smug resident of the impregnable ivory tower of thought respond when *his* faith is tested? Watch and see, Lewis implies; and *A Grief Observed* is the answer. But there is internal evidence, as well as antecedents in Lewis's work (see his Five Sonnets, for example) and contemporaneous letters and conversations, that show a sophisticated understanding of its rhetorical potential.

No one, not even C. S. Lewis, writes serial diary entries that combine into a beginning, middle, and end, with the climax, a near-loss-of-faith-*cum*-rage, at the very center, rising thereafter into an emotionally reformulated—but not, since none was genuinely lost, recovered—faith. Diaries do not discover and dispose issues as neatly as they are discovered and disposed in, say, *Miracles*. Was Lewis really tempted to consult mediums so as to contact the spirit of his dead wife—just as many others have been tempted? Was Lewis the enthusiastic Club man he seems in the book? Would phrases, such as "fear-fulfillment," used elsewhere, appear here whole? An inventory of Lewisian ideas—the Law of Inattention, God not ignoring but waiving our questions until we know what we are talking about (until we have a "face"), love as a surrendering of the self as to a dance—all appear. The book, the last autobiography, is no break with, but rather a complement to, everything else he had written, right down to his use of himself as a *datum*, though now with characteristic obliqueness.

None of this is to say that there is anything theologically, emotionally, or psychologically false about the book. Certainly Lewis's love for Joy, the depth of his loss upon her death, and the severity of his grief as a result, are not at issue. The book is true in all the important senses. But Lewis had much, finally, to grieve over in addition to Joy's death and knew that the rest of us do, too. He so loved her that he could truthfully say to his friend Nevill Coghill, "I never expected to have, in my sixties, the happiness that passed me by in my twenties," and mean wholly "passed by" and wholly "have." (Some have raised a question regarding the consummation of the marriage, but I have none.) His surprise, though, cannot be ours. The romance and marriage were simply the end of one more delay brought on by his mother's death, just as is the great motif of *The Magician's Nephew*.

Digory Kirke's mother is near death, and Digory can do nothing about it. Nothing, that is, until, after considerable misadventure of the gravest consequence, he comes upon an apple, in a walled garden, atop a hill, in the newly-created world of Narnia. He knows that Aslan—who of course created Narnia and whom Digory has seen cry great tears on behalf of his stricken mother, as though the Lion felt more grief than the boy himself—has sent him to retrieve that fruit but to take none of it. But in the garden he finds the Witch, whose presence in the yet-unfallen world he is responsible for, and she truly tells him that the smallest piece of an apple from a certain tree will cure his mother. The temptation is excruciating, but Digory obeys, doing as he has been bidden. When he returns to Aslan, the Lion gives the boy a small slice of the apple to take back to earth for his mother to eat:

> He peeled it and cut it up and gave it to her piece by piece. And no sooner had she finished it than she smiled and her head sank back on the pillow and she was asleep: a real, natural, gentle sleep, without any of those nasty drugs, which was, as Digory knew, the thing in the whole world that she wanted most. And he was sure now that her face looked a little different. He bent down and kissed her very softly, and stole out of the room with a beating heart. . . . About a week after this it was quite certain that Digory's mother was getting better.

Presently Digory learns that his father, who had been away in India, was to return home "forever and ever . . . and the great big house in the country, which Digory had heard of all his life and never seen, would now be their home." He had already learned that had he stolen the apple for his mother she would have lived, but that her life would have had consequences so terrible that everyone would have regretted the theft.

The fictional episode scarcely wants commentary, so tellingly close to the biographical one are its details. The entire traumatic event of Flora's death was recapitulated, precisely as the literature of parental loss predicts it must be if delay is to end. The entire event, except for the ending, was changed by a son who saw it differently, now in a much larger context, without which there is no fixed or reliable meaning. At the end of his book Beversluis writes that the crisis of *A Grief Observed* was "a crisis in meaning." The better critique of *A Grief Observed*—perhaps the best, as of *The Magician's Nephew* and *Surprised by Joy*—is in a 1527 sermon by Martin Luther: "When God wants to strengthen a man's faith he first weakens it by feigning to break faith with him. He thrusts him into many tribulations. . . so that when God returns to him and lets the sun shine again . . . he opens his eyes in amazement and says 'God dwells here'."

III

Not only is Orual's complaint her *Surprised by Joy*, with its incumbent distortions and concealments of self, but we can profitably view *A Grief Observed* as Lewis's own complaint, soon after which, though not immediately like Orual, he dies. In short, there is recapitulation on a higher scale than that adumbrated in *The Magician's Nephew*: Once delay ends, most of what follows is recapitulation. Just as Lewis had gotten it all wrong in prematurely rushing himself to husband a household with Mrs. Moore, he got it exactly right in finding, loving, marrying, and succoring Joy. Just as—shall I call that which follows the end of delay "rebirth"?—the "re-definition of self" begins with Digory's most affecting and necessary recapitulation, so it is marked by that putting aside of the rhetorical self, and then perfectly punctuated by the twin proclamations of *A Grief Observed* descending (with an incipient rise) and the affirming, settled, and redemptive glory of *Letters to Malcolm*. Thus, along the lines of Sir Thomas Browne's *Religio Medici*, which reconciled the inquiring skepticism of a scientist with his deep and orthodox religious faith, Lewis has wrought a *Rhetorica Religii*, the sort of thing that Kenneth Burke demotes to mere "logology" but which St. Augustine—a keen, zealous, and professional rhetorician, let us remember—approximated as he sought to celebrate "signs of divine presence within the human mind," as Eustace and Jill, with Puddleglum's proclamatory help of course, come to understand in *The Silver Chair*.

As I suggested very early on, this stage of Lewis's work places him within a constellation of writers with whom he is not ordinarily associated. But Walker Percy, especially his *The Second Coming* and *The Thanatos Syndrome*; Robertson Davies, his *Fifth Business* in particular; Sigrid Undset, the Nobel Prize winner whose *Kristin Lavrensdatter* is so woefully neglected; and Thornton Wilder, whose *The Bridge of San Luis Rey* is taken for granted and whose *The Eighth Day* is the "great American novel"—along with others, of course—have written the same sort of sacramentally oblique work as Lewis, who I wish had done it more. They—but especially Undset—understand the world to be haunted, that meaning is everywhere, and that we must learn to read the signs.

So it is not a new rhetoric, *but it is an existential one*, which by now should seem less odd to us than it would to C. S. Lewis, who had no patience with Existentialism or, as I have indicated, with such of its embodiments as Kierkegaard, whom he dismissed with exclamatory impatience. But Lewis was wrong, as I believe he was wrong about his atheism, about Orual, about rhetoric in general, and about Albert. His rejection may have been preponderantly tonal. In his "Three Kinds of Men," for example, he describes those who seek pleasure, others who acknowledge a higher claim upon them, and a third for whom, like St. Paul, "to live is Christ." The burden of proof is on the defense to show how this taxonomy is *not* Kierkegaard's aesthetic, ethical, and religious stages, that Lewis was *not* a Knight of Faith incarnate, rejecting the crowd to follow God whatever the price, and that Lewis did *not* live a dialectic that found selfhood not a given, but dependent upon reading the signs and choosing to follow them.

Especially the burden of proof is on the defense to show that he did not come to rely more and more heavily on Kierkegaard's notion of "indirect communication," what I have called oblique or, more particularly, veiled discourse. I know that this analysis, like any, can be pushed too far. I am not now suggesting Kierkegaard was either a source or an influence, though he may have been both, but rather using him as a touchstone: the Dane used indirect communications early, rather than late, in his career and often with an irony not found in the Lewis works of the period in question. The many dissimilarities between Lewis and avowed, or acknowledged, existentialist writers can be adduced. Overemphasis on the irrational, for example, or the very fact that he might be grouped with Sartre brings on a bad case of hives, but there are sub-categories of existentialist writers as there are of any other category. Perhaps that possibility accounts for an exchange I had with Paul Holmer (see his "Kierkegaard, a Religious Author," in the *American-Scandinavian Review*, vol. 33 [June 1945], pp. 147-52). When I asked him if Lewis was, after all, an existential writer, he answered, "If you want him to be." Or even if you do not.

Beversluis writes that the crisis of *A Grief Observed* is a "crisis of meaning," and he is almost right. There was such a crisis; but it was not over Joy's death, and it had come some ten years earlier. If Lewis as an existential writer is odd, is it not odder still that a man in his early fifties, a man who had been a professing, orthodox, virtuous Christian for twenty years and for over a dozen of those the foremost Christian voice in the English-speaking world, a man, yet, who had written an essay, "On Forgiveness," in his late forties in which he warned, "To refuse it is to refuse God's mercy for ourselves," is it not very odd indeed that *this man did not believe that his own sins were forgiven?* On St. Stephen's Day, December 26, 1951, he wrote in a letter, "as for myself a great joy has befallen me. Difficult though this is, I shall try to explain this in words." He continues: "For a long time I believed that I believed in the forgiveness of sins. But suddenly (on St. Mark's day [April 25]) this truth appeared in mind in so clear a light that I perceived that never before (and that after many confessions and absolutions) had I believed it with my whole heart. So great is the difference between mere affirmation by the intellect and that faith, fixed in the very marrow and as it were palpable, which the Apostle wrote was *substance*." He had written to Arthur in 1936 that he found "the lion of strength" in Charles Williams's *The Place of the Lion* not only "exciting fantasy" but "deeply religious." Why? Because it showed the workings of intellectual abuse and thus taught him "more than I ever knew yet about humility." It is no wonder that Lewis never published the essay.

The correspondent is Fr. Giovanni Calabria, an Italian priest with whom Lewis would exchange letters from 1947 until Fr. Calabria's death in December of 1954; their language was Latin, the only one both held comfortably in common. This affirmation, astonishing in that it had to be made at all, let alone at such a late date, is not alone among the confessions Lewis makes to the priest. On January 14, 1949, he wrote, "I feel my zeal for writing, and whatever talent I originally possessed, to be decreasing; nor (I believe) do I please my readers as I used to. I labour under many difficulties. My house is unquiet and devastated by women's quarrels. . . . My aged mother, worn out by long infirmity, is my daily care." He then concludes his meditation with, "If it shall please God that I write more books, blessed be He. If it shall not please Him, again, blessed be He. Perhaps it will be the most wholesome thing for my soul that I lose both fame and skill lest I were to fall into that evil disease, vainglory." Nine months later the gloom seems to have deepened. In explaining a long delay in responding to a letter from Fr. Calabria, Lewis diagnoses as his own an utterly incredible spiritual disease. "For nothing else was responsible for it except the perpetual labour of writing and (lest I should seem to exonerate myself too much) a certain Accidia"—Lewis was, he thought, slothful; Lewis, lazy at writing and thus afflicted by "an evil disease and, I believe, of the Seven Deadly Sins that one which in me is the strongest—though few believe this of me."

This correspondence is unlike anything else in Lewis. Always revealing, routinely edifying, and frequently deeply moving, its great charm lies in the affection and respect that the men share for each other. Its intimacy so engages the reader that Fr. Calabria's death comes as a blow. It would repay close study; but our interest is in chronology. Nineteen forty-nine was clearly a low point for Lewis, who thought he would write no more, welcomed the possibility as an antidote to what must have been a besetting temptation, thought himself lazy to the point of sinfulness, and did not in his heart believe his sins were forgiven. Furthermore, he was tormented by a domestic intranquility largely the doing of Mrs. Moore. Two years later, at the end of 1951, his sins are forgiven; and of course he would overflow with an expository and an imaginative effusion that would suffice for a handful of entire careers. Rhetoric, the faculty as well as the art, especially an existential rhetoric faithfully played out, is "epistemic" and, as it happens, symptomatic as well.

What happened, and what I believe made all the difference, was death. In the summer of 1948, Mrs. Moore had retired permanently to a nursing home; by March of 1949, some nine months later but before he writes of his *accidia*, Lewis had completed the manuscript of *The Lion, the Witch and the Wardrobe*, long in gestation, as was the case with many of his books. The rest of that year he would spend in the gloom that he confesses to the priest. Then, a little more than a year thereafter, Mrs. Moore died, on January 12, 1951. Before the year is out he knows his sins are forgiven; and here begins the rebirth, that redefinition of self that alters his rhetoric. In "On Forgiveness," he insists upon the condition of God's forgiveness, saying that He has left us no choice, namely, that we forgive those who have trespassed against us. Perhaps only in early 1951, after the departure of a daily reminder of great and reciprocal sin was he able to forgive Mrs. Moore. After all, he had written in "On Forgiveness" that the mere passage of time is meaningless if a long-ago sin remains truly unrepented.

So if there was a mystery, as some have felt, it resided in an odd asynchronicity brought on by the delay of early parental loss and by the need for some sort of recapitulation thus to set things right. But before he (or any of us) could do that, what has been set wrong must be cleared away. Just as a physician does when he re-breaks a badly mended bone in order to set it properly; and just as Lewis did publicly, by his massive, varied, and organic refutation of a pathological zeitgeist:

one marked by an atavistic nineteenth-century determinism and a *soi-disant* postmodern, acontextual self-indulgence. But where clearing away mattered most was, of course, in the enduring Deeper life, the transcendence of will, and the reconciliation of the many selves, as delay ended and the Unknown Self grew into the Open. His distortions of personality had begun shortly after Flora's death, when he became a putative atheist; his recovery—that is, his conversion—occurred not long after Albert's. The delay ended, forgiveness was given and granted, despair overcome, and re-definition of both the rhetorical voice and of the Deeper life undertaken after the death of Mrs. Moore and all she must have signified. Then he rose into a refreshened faith upon his recovery from the grief of Joy's death. Yet it was not easy for Lewis to get right. The geniuses that would do the proving had themselves been proven.

Silence

"THE SEEING EYE" is the last essay in the second post-humous collection that Walter Hooper edited, *Christian Reflections*, and it is, I think, among Lewis's most useful. In it he ponders the assertion that Russian astronauts have not found God in outer space and goes on to say things which, typically, seem manifestly self-evident—*after* he has said them, of course, but also said them almost peripherally. "If God created the universe, He created space-time"—so far, so obvious. But next comes the *subordinate clause*: "which is to the universe as the metre is to a poem or the key is to music." Well, of course! That *certainly is* space-time. (All along there is a familiar small, soft voice, at least in my head, whispering, "so *that's* space-time.") Hence, Lewis continues, "to look for Him as one item within the framework which He Himself invented is nonsensical." After all, he adds, "a fish is no more, and no less, in the sea"—here he will drive the point home—"after it has swum a thousand miles than it was when it set out. . . . To some, God is discoverable everywhere; to others, nowhere. Those who do not find Him on earth are unlikely to find Him in space. . . ." He concludes, "Much depends on the seeing eye"—just as seeing the poem instead of merely squiggly lines does.

To have a seeing eye—knowing that there is a poem to be seen—may require a leap of faith, a quintessentially existential choice; and there exists an idea that might justify it. It is John Henry Cardinal Newman's Illative Sense, unaccountably neglected by philosophers and rhetoricians alike. First we doubt, says Newman in his *An Essay in Aid of a Grammar of Assent*, then we infer, and finally we assent, first notionally, then assertively—that is, really—a "supra-logical judgment," which closely resembles a claim for Divine participation, warranted by Logos. This last occurs when finally we recognize *meaning*, whether ratiocinatively or imaginatively, and thus truth—the way things are (e.g., natural law). Although it develops as a habit, it originates in our nature, he says, like "good sense," "common sense," or a "sense of beauty." In other words, it conveys us across the gaps that separate evidence from conclusion and both from some warrant; it is the "therefore" and the "since" adumbrated earlier. Could there be any more accurate a paradigm for the life and rhetoric of C. S. Lewis? When the Man of Letters speaks with *auctoritee* on myth, metaphor, and meaning in language and literature; or the Apologist reasons; or the preacher and romancer beckons; or the fellow fugitive reflects, wonders, confesses, and suggests; or the maieutic rhetorician in his many incarnations does not say "think this" or "this is true" but, as Debra Winger suggests, "think of this" or try it this way, then he is speaking illatively, his "extension of natural conversation" sufficiently inviting so as to convey us across the gaps. This is no "flashy rhetoric" or "trumpery," but a nuanced, thoughtful, committed religious thinker "speaking well."

Lewis's geniuses—that combination of will and vocation, militant intellect, and rhetorical temper; of spiritual attentiveness to reading, thinking, and experience; and of the struggle with loss, not only of his parents but of Paddy and of the life-saving sergeant and of Charles Williams and of his brother to alcoholism, and of Joy; of the whole dialectic of self-discovery, of self-bondage, and then, as the Thin Woman understood, of liberation—Lewis's geniuses, all in the greater company of Providential design ("Let us not reckon without our host"), had guided him truly after all. Percy, whose summary of Christian existentialism is perfectly applicable to the author of *A Grief Observed,* provides a more suggestive, but characteristically slanted, answer: "Existentialism has taught us that what man is cannot be grasped by the science of man. The case is rather that man's science is one of the things that man does, a mode of existence. *Another mode is speech.* Man is not merely a higher organism responding to and controlling his environment. He is . . . that being in the world whose calling it is to find a name for Being, to give testimony to it, and to provide for it a clearing [emphasis added]." For "speech" we may substitute "rhetoric," the faculty that is *epistemic.*

In "Christianity and Literature," a paper from the thirties, Lewis noted that "a cultured person . . . is almost compelled to be aware that reality is very odd and that the ultimate truth, whatever it may be, *must* have the characteristics of strangeness—*must* be something that would seem remote and fantastic to the uncultured." Or, as Percy has put it, we are shipwrecked and await "the message in the bottle," one that a seeing eye discerns and only the *Homo rhetoricus* can translate for the rest of us. That is why I have always thought that a couplet from Alexander Pope's *An Essay on Criticism* gets it just right when applied to Lewis and his world of discourse:

> *Something, whose truth convinced at sight we find,*
> *That gives us back the image of our mind.*

Finally, like Orual we at least consider crossing the greatest gap of all, to that "clearing" in which Being has been named. In his commentary on Galatians, Luther taught, though in a polemical context, what Lewis surely came dearly to hold and to teach: "This is the reason why our theology is certain: It snatches us away from ourselves, so that we do not depend on our own strength; conscience, experience, person, or works but depend on that which is outside ourselves, that is, on the promise and truth of God, which cannot deceive." Not that which "works" but that which is true—that which because of its coherence reveals meaning in the apparently meaningless— ought to win our assent. The establishment of meaning—an interconnected wholeness and a renewed confidence in our ability to apprehend it—was the basis of Lewis's conversion and became the basis of his "apologetic" appeal.

The last line of the diary, *All My Road Before Me*, reads, "is there never to be any peace or comfort?" Not very long thereafter he had learned the answer. Confiding to Arthur he wrote,

> [Barfield] said among other things that he thought the idea of the spiritual world as *home*—the discovery of homeliness in that which is otherwise so remote—the feeling that you are coming *back* tho' to a place you have never yet reached—was peculiar to the British, and thought that MacDonald, Chesterton, and I, had this more than anyone else. He doesn't know you of course. . . . [T]hat is another of the beauties of coming, I won't say, to religion, but to an attempt at religion—one finds one- self on the main road with all humanity, and can com- pare notes with an endless succession of previous

travellers. It is emphatically coming home: as Chaucer says 'Returneth *home* from worldly vanitee.'

What he irresistibly shows us at the very end of *The Chronicles of Narnia* vindicates Barfield's judgment:

[T]hey found themselves all walking together — and a great, bright procession it was — up towards mountains higher than you could see in this world even if they were there to be seen. But there was no snow on those mountains: there were forests and greens slopes and sweet orchards and flashing waterfalls, one above the other, going up forever. And the land they were walking on grew narrower all the time, with a deep valley on each side: and across that valley the land which was the real England grew nearer and nearer.

Having seen where Lewis was born and raised, I cannot help seeing Ireland, nor disbelieving that he meant it, too. Warren, who loved walking and talking and Ireland as much as Jack, and home even more, surely understood, as would have Mammy and Pappy. We devoted beneficiaries of his great achievement must be grateful that he took that road and traveled it, as Chesterton had written of his pilgrim, "round the whole world till [he] came back to the same place."

So he was not routinely homesick when he wrote to Arthur as early as March 30, 1915, of the feeling of "estrangement" which he never quite got over when in "a foreign country." (He thinks he means England.) Rather, he was prescient, or in the hands of that "second cause" cited earlier. The nuisances and estrangement serve, he says, "as a delightful reminder of how different it will all be soon. Already one's mind dwells upon the sights and sound and smells of home. . .". Where else but back home would a fugitive pilgrim be headed? Peter Bayley was a pupil, and later friend, of C. S. Lewis. He closes his memoir of his old tutor by recalling his funeral at Headington Quarry, "on a very cold, frosty but brilliantly sunny November morning." Bayley concludes: "There was one candle on the coffin as it was carried out into the churchyard. It seemed not only appropriate but almost a symbol of the man and his integrity and his absoluteness and his faith that the flame burned so steadily, even in the open air, and seemed so bright, even in the bright sun."

"We have lost a friend," said James Dundas-Grant to Lewis's physician, Dr. Havard, who answered quietly, "Only for a time, D.G." Who but James Stephens could best tell us what happens next? Finally, the crock of gold returned, the gods both wild and tame having taken a hand, the Thin Woman and others go to fetch her husband, and then,

> They swept through the goat tracks and the little boreens and the curving roads. Down to the city they went dancing and singing; among the streets and the shops telling their sunny tale; not heeding the malignant eyes.... And they took the philosopher from his prison, even the Intellect of Man they took from the hands of the doctors and lawyers, from the sly priests, from the professors whose mouths are gorged with sawdust, and the merchants who sell blades of grass ... and then they returned again, dancing and singing, to the country of the gods....

A Brief Chronology

THE SOURCES OF THIS CHRONOLOGY are various, the most thorough being Green and Hooper, *C. S. Lewis: A Biography*. An indispensable adjunct to any Lewis chronology is that on Warren Lewis found in Kilby and Mead, *Brothers and Friends: The Diaries of Major Warren Hamilton Lewis*. For a bibliographic chronology, the reader is referred to "Works Consulted", where Lewis's books are listed in their order of publication.

1862   Florence ("Flora") Augusta Hamilton, C. S. Lewis's mother and one of four children, born to Thomas Hamilton and Mary Warren. She will win Honors in algebra and geometry in 1880, then in logic and mathematics in 1885, from Queen's College, Belfast.

1863   Albert James Lewis (solicitor), C. S. Lewis's father and one of six children, born to Richard Lewis and Martha Gee in Cork, Ireland.

1872   Janie King Moore (Askins), "Minto," Lewis's companion, "adopted mother," and mother of Maureen and Paddy Moore, born.

1895   Warren Hamilton Lewis, C. S. Lewis's brother and dearest friend; soldier, historian of seventeenth-century France, editor, and diarist, born. (Joseph) Arthur Greeves, Lewis's Belfast neighbor and lifelong friend, born.

1898   Edward Francis Courtenay Moore, "Paddy," Lewis's bunkmate and brother-in-arms, born.

1898   CLIVE STAPLES LEWIS BORN, NOVEMBER 29.

1905   The prospering Lewis family moves to a new house, "Little Lea" in County Down.

1906   Maureen Daisy Helen Moore, Lewis's "adopted sister" (the late Lady Dunbar Of Hempriggs), born.

1908   Flora Lewis dies, August 23.

1911   AT SCHOOL IN ENGLAND, LEWIS CEASES TO BE A CHRISTIAN.

1914   Lewis begins private tutoring with W. T. Kirkpatrick (1848-1921), a severe dialectician and atheist, for whom Lewis will develop great affection.

1915   (Helen) Joy Davidman, later Mrs. C. S. Lewis, born, Bronx, New York.

1917-19   Though accepted to Oxford, Lewis enlists in the army and spends his nineteenth birthday in the trenches. After suffering trench fever he returns to action, takes prisoners, and is wounded in battle. Paddy Moore killed in action in 1918.

1919   Lewis returns to University College and establishes a household with Maureen and Mrs. Moore, with whom he visited before his departure to France.

1925   After winning three firsts (philosophy, 1920; classics, 1922; English literature, 1923) and substituting for E. F. Carritt as a philosophy tutor for one year at University College, Lewis is elected to a fellowship in English language and literature at Magdalen College.

1929   Albert Lewis dies, September 24. Shortly thereafter Lewis returns to a belief in God, though not yet in Christ.

1930   The Lewis brothers, Warren now retired from the army, and the Moores purchase and move into the Kilns, in Headington Quarry, just outside Oxford. Maureen will leave the household in 1941, when she marries Leonard Blake.

1931   C. S. LEWIS BECOMES A CHRISTIAN and learns that Warren, quite independently, has also converted to the Faith.

1933-50 Lewis most active as author and speaker. Friendships flourish with the Inklings and on walking tours, and he achieves great fame and earns several honors. The following items suggest the varied richness of this period: BBC broadcasts (Aug. 1941, Jan.-Feb. 1942, Sept.-Nov. 1942, Feb.-Apr. 1944); Socratic Club presidency (1941-54); publication of some fifteen books of apologetics, fiction, and scholarship. Of particular interest are his meeting with Charles Williams (b. 1886) in 1936, Williams's death in 1945, and the publication of *The Screwtape Letters* in 1942. The latter (along with his BBC talks) brings Lewis his greatest fame, an enormous correspondence, and his picture on the cover of *Time* magazine (September 8, 1947). In September of 1947 he enters into a Latin correspondence with Don Giovanni Calabria, an Italian priest, which will last until the latter's death in 1954. In the summer of 1948, Mrs. Moore retires permanently to a nursing home, and by March of 1949 Lewis has completed the manuscript of *The Lion, the Witch and the*

Wardrobe, which will be published in 1950. The remaining
six books of *The Chronicles of Narnia* will be published
annually through 1956, the same year in which *Till We
Have Faces*, his only novel and surely his greatest fiction,
is published as well.

1951   Janie King Moore dies, January 12. Lewis declines the
honor of being named commander of the Order of the
British Empire.

1952-53 Lewis and Joy Davidman (Gresham) meet in September,
after having corresponded at length. In January of 1953,
Joy returns to the United States; then again, in December, she comes to England, this time with her two young
sons.

1954   Lewis is elected professor of Medieval and Renaissance
English literature at Magdalene College, Cambridge.

1955   He assumes the Professorial Chair.

1956-58 Lewis and Joy Davidman are married at the Oxford registry office (April 23, 1956); by November she is near death
from a recurrence of cancer; in response to her request,
Lewis marries Joy in a bedside ecclesiastical ceremony
(March 27, 1957). By December Joy is walking again. In
June of 1958, Joy's cancer is arrested, and in July the couple
honeymoon in Ireland.

1960   Three months after a physically painful trip to Greece
with Lewis, Joy Davidman Lewis dies, July 13.

1963   C. S. LEWIS DIES, NOVEMBER 22.

1966   Arthur Greeves dies, August 29.

1973   Warren Lewis dies, April 19.

Works Consulted

SELECTED WORKS OF C. S. LEWIS (listed chronologically)

Lewis Family Papers: Memoirs of the Lewis Family, 1850-1930. Com. and ed. Warren Lewis. Deposited at the Wade Center, Wheaton College and at the Bodleian Library, Oxford University.

Spirits in Bondage: A Cycle of Lyrics. London: William Heinemann, 1919.

Dymer. London: J. N. Dent, 1926.

The Pilgrim's Regress: An Allegorical Apology for Christianity, Reason and Romanticism. London: J. N. Dent, 1933.

The Allegory of Love: A Study in Medieval Tradition. Oxford: Clarendon Press, 1936.

Out of the Silent Planet. London: John Lane The Bodley Head, 1938.

Rehabilitations: And Other Essays. London: Oxford University Press, 1939.

The Personal Heresy: A Controversy. With E. M. W. Tillyard. London: Oxford University Press, 1939.

The Problem of Pain. London: The Centenary Press, 1940.

The Screwtape Letters. London: Geoffrey Bles, 1942.

Preface to Paradise Lost. London: Oxford University Press, 1942.

Perelandra. London: The Bodley Head, 1943.

The Abolition of Man, or Reflections on Education with Special
    Reference to the Teaching of English in the Upper Forms of
    Schools. London: Oxford University Press, 1943.
That Hideous Strength. London: John Lane The Bodley Head, 1945.
The Great Divorce: A Dream. London: Geoffrey Bles: The Cente-
    nary Press, 1945.
Miracles: A Preliminary Study. London: Geoffrey Bles: The Cen-
    tenary Press, 1947. London: Collins, Fontana Books, 1960.
Transposition: And Other Addresses. London: Geoffrey Bles, 1949.
The Lion, the Witch and the Wardrobe. London: Geoffrey Bles, 1950.
Prince Caspian. London: Geoffrey Bles, 1951.
Mere Christianity. London: Geoffrey Bles, 1952.
The Voyage of the Dawn Treader. London: Geoffrey Bles, 1952.
The Silver Chair. London: Geoffrey Bles, 1953.
The Horse and His Boy. London: Geoffrey Bles, 1954.
English Literature in the Sixteenth Century, Excluding Drama.
    Oxford: Clarendon Press, 1954.
The Magician's Nephew. London: The Bodley Head, 1955.
Surprised by Joy: The Shape of My Early Life. London: Geoffrey
    Bles, 1955.
The Last Battle. London: The Bodley Head, 1956.
Till We Have Faces: A Myth Retold. London: Geoffrey Bles, 1956.
Reflections on the Psalms. London: Geoffrey Bles, 1958.
The Four Loves. London: Geoffrey Bles, 1960.
Studies in Words. Cambridge: Cambridge University Press, 1960.
The World's Last Night: And Other Essays. New York: Harcourt,
    Brace & Co., 1960.
A Grief Observed. London: Faber and Faber, 1961.
An Experiment in Criticism. Cambridge: Cambridge University
    Press, 1961.
They Asked for a Paper: Papers and Addresses. London: Geoffrey
    Bles, 1962.
Letters to Malcolm: Chiefly On Prayer. London: Geoffrey Bles, 1964.
The Discarded Image: An Introduction to Medieval and Renaissance
    Literature. Cambridge: Cambridge University Press, 1964.

Poems. Ed. Walter Hooper. London: Geoffrey Bles, 1964.

Screwtape Proposes a Toast, and Other Pieces. London: Collins, Fontana Paperbacks, 1965.

Studies in Medieval and Renaissance Literature. Collected by Walter Hooper. Cambridge: Cambridge University Press, 1966.

Letters of C. S. Lewis. Ed., with a Memoir, W. H. Lewis. London: Geoffrey Bles, 1966.

Of Other Worlds: Essays and Stories. Ed. Walter Hooper. London: Geoffrey Bles, 1966.

Christian Reflections. Ed. Walter Hooper. London: Geoffrey Bles, 1967.

Letters to an American Lady. Ed. Clyde S. Kilby. Grand Rapids: Wm. B. Eerdmans, 1967.

Narrative Poems. Ed. Walter Hooper. London: Geoffrey Bles, 1969.

Selected Literary Essays. Ed. Walter Hooper. Cambridge: Cambridge University Press, 1969.

God in the Dock. Ed. Walter Hooper. Grand Rapids: Wm. B. Eerdmans, 1970.

Fern-seed and Elephants. Ed. Walter Hooper. London: Collins, Fontana Paperbacks, 1975.

The Dark Tower & Other Stories. Ed. Walter Hooper. London: Collins, 1977.

They Stand Together: The Letters of C. S. Lewis to Arthur Greeves (1914-1963). Ed. Walter Hooper. London: Collins, 1979; New York: Macmillan, 1979.

Of This and Other Worlds. Ed. Walter Hooper. London: Collins, 1982.

Boxen. Ed. Walter Hooper. London: Collins, 1985.

Letters to Children. Ed. Lyle W. Dorsett and Marjorie Lamp Mead. New York: Macmillan, 1985.

Present Concerns. Eds. Walter Hooper. London: Collins, 1986.

Letters: C. S. Lewis, Don Giovanni Calabria: A Study in Friendship. Trans. and ed. Martin Moynihan. London: Collins, 1989.

Christian Reunion And Other Essays. Ed. Walter Hooper. London: Collins, Fount Paperback, 1990.

All My Road Before Me: The Diary of C. S. Lewis 1922-27. London: HarperCollins, 1991.

WORKS ABOUT C. S. LEWIS

Adey, Lionel. *C. S. Lewis's "Great War" with Owen Barfield.* English Literary Studies Monograph Series No. 14. University of Victoria, B.C., Canada: 1978.

Aeschliman, Michael D. *The Restitution of Man: C. S. Lewis and the Case Against Scientism.* Grand Rapids: Wm. B. Eerdmans, 1983.

Barfield, Owen. *Owen Barfield on C. S. Lewis.* Ed. G. B. Tennyson. Middletown: Wesleyan University Press, 1989.

Berryman, J.A.N. In *Books* 1 October 1939: 18.

Beversluis, John. *C. S. Lewis and the Search for Rational Religion.* Grand Rapids: Wm. B. Eerdmans, 1985.

Carnell, Corbin Scott. *Bright Shadows of Reality: C. S. Lewis and the Feeling Intellect.* Grand Rapids: Wm. B. Eerdmans, 1974.

Christopher, Joe R. *C. S. Lewis.* Twayne's English Authors Series. Boston: Twayne Publishers, 1996.

_____, and Joan K. Ostling. *C. S. Lewis: An Annotated Checklist About Him and His Works.* The Serif Series: No. 30, Bibliographies and Checklists. Kent: Kent State University Press, 1973.

Como, James T., ed. *'C. S. Lewis at the Breakfast Table' and Other Reminiscences.* San Diego: Harcourt Brace Jovanovich, 1992.

"C. S. Lewis Goes Marching On." *Time.* 5 December 1977, 92.

Cunningham, Richard B. *C. S. Lewis: Defender of the Faith.* Philadelphia: The Westminster Press, 1967.

Derrick, Christopher. *C. S. Lewis and the Church of Rome.* San Francisco: Ignatius Press, 1981.

Empson, William. In *The Spectator,* CLVII (4 September 1936), 950.

Essays on C. S. Lewis and George MacDonald: Truth, Fiction and the Power of Imagination. Studies in British Literature. Lewiston, N.Y.: Edwin Mellen Press, n.d.

Gibb, Jocelyn, ed. *Light on C. S. Lewis.* New York: Harcourt, Brace & World, 1965.

Gofar, Janine, comp. and ed. *C. S. Lewis Index: Rumours from the Sculptor's Shop.* Riverside: La Sierra University Press, 1995.

Green, Roger Lancelyn, and Walter Hooper. *C. S. Lewis: A Biography.* London: Collins, 1974.

Gresham, Douglas. *Lenten Lands: My Childhood with Joy Davidman and C. S. Lewis.* New York: Macmillan, 1988.

Hannay, Margaret Patterson. *C. S. Lewis.* New York: Frederick Ungar Publishing Company, 1981.

Harries, Richard. *C. S. Lewis: The Man and His God.* Wilton, Conn.: Morehouse-Barlow, 1987.

Hart, D. A. "C. S. Lewis's Defense of Poesie." Ph.d diss., University of Wisconsin, 1960.

Holmer, Paul L. *C. S. Lewis: The Shape of His Faith and Thought.* New York: Harper & Row, 1976.

Hooper, Walter. *C. S. Lewis: A Companion and Guide.* London: HarperCollins, 1996.

_____. *Past Watchful Dragons.* London: Collier Macmillan, 1971.

Howard, Thomas. *C. S. Lewis: Man of Letters.* San Francisco: Ignatius Press, 1987.

Huttar, Charles, ed. *Imagination and the Spirit: Essays in Literature and the Christian Faith Presented to Clyde S. Kilby.* Grand Rapids: Wm. B. Eerdmans, 1971.

Keefe, Carolyn, ed. *C. S. Lewis, Speaker and Teacher.* Grand Rapids: Zondervan Press, 1971.

Kilby, Clyde S. *The Christian World of C. S. Lewis.* Grand Rapids: Wm. B. Eerdmans, 1964.

Lowenberg, Susan. *C. S. Lewis: A Reference Guide, 1972-1988.* New York: G. K. Hall & Co., 1993.

MacDonald, Michael H., and Andrew A. Tadie, eds. *The Riddle of Joy: G. K. Chesterton and C. S. Lewis.* Grand Rapids: Wm. B. Eerdmans, 1989.

Manlove, C. N. *C. S. Lewis: His Literary Achievement.* New York: St. Martin's Press, 1987.

Meilaender, Gilbert. *The Taste for the Other: The Social and Ethical Thought of C. S. Lewis.* Grand Rapids: Wm. B. Eerdmans, 1978.

Menuge, Angus J. L., ed. *C. S. Lewis—Lightbearer in the Shadowlands: The Evangelistic Vision of C. S. Lewis.* Wheaton: Crossway Books, 1997.

Nakao, Sister Setsko, A.C.J. "The Pilgrim's Regress: A Way of Detachment." *The Bulletin of Seisen University* 32 (1984): 1-15.

_____. "Salvation Theme in *Till We Have Faces.*" *The Bulletin of Seisen University* 31 (1983): 21-33.

Patrick, James. *The Magdalen Metaphysicals: Idealism and Orthodoxy at Oxford, 1901-1945.* Macon, Georgia: Mercer University Press, 1985.

Purtill, Richard L. *C. S. Lewis's Case for the Christianity.* San Francisco: Harper & Row, 1981.

Sayer, George. *Jack: C. S. Lewis and His Times.* San Francisco: Harper & Row, 1988.

Schakel, Peter J., ed. *The Longing for a Form.* Kent: The Kent State University Press, 1977.

_____, and Charles A. Huttar, edd. *Word and Story in C. S. Lewis.* Columbia: University of Missouri Press, 1991.

Schofield, Stephen, ed. *In Search of C. S. Lewis.* South Plainfield: Bridge Publishing, 1983.

Shiels, Merrill. "Chuck Colson's Leveler," *Time.* 9 September 1974.

The Times of London. 6 June 1936, 475.

The Times of London. 17 September 1954, 592.

Walker, Dr. Andrew, and Dr. James Patrick, eds. *A Christian for All Christians: Essays in Honor of C. S. Lewis.* Washington: Regnery Gateway, 1992.

Walsh, Chad. *The Literary Legacy of C. S. Lewis.* New York: Harcourt Brace Jovanovich, 1979.

Watson, George, ed. *Critical Essays on C. S. Lewis.* Critical Series: I. Aldershot, England: Scolar Press, 1992.

White, William Luther. *The Image of Man in C. S. Lewis.* Nashville: Abingdon Press, 1969.

Willis, John Randolph, S.J. *Pleasure Forevermore: The Theology of C. S. Lewis*. Chicago: Loyola University Press, 1983.

Wilson, A. N. *C. S. Lewis: A Biography*. New York: Fawcett Columbine, 1990.

OTHER WORKS

A Kempis, Thomas. *The Imitation of Christ*. Trans. Leo Sherley-Price. Harmondsworth: Penguin Books, 1952.

Altschul, Sol, ed. *Childhood Bereavement and Its Aftermath*. Emotions and Behavior Monographs: Monograph No. 8. Madison, Conn.: International Universities Press, Inc., 1988.

Anscombe, G. E. M. *Metaphysics and the Philosophy of Mind*. Vol. II, *The Collected Philsophical Papers of G. E. M. Anscombe*. Minneapolis: University of Minnesota Press, 1981.

Anstey, F. *Humour and Fantasy: Vice Versa*. 1882. London: John Murray, 1931.

Barfield, Owen. *History in English Words*. London: Faber and Faber Ltd., 1953.

_____. *Poetic Diction: A Study in Meaning*. 1928. 3rd ed. Middletown: Wesleyan University Press, 1973.

Barth, Karl. *Homiletics*. Trans. EVZ-Verlag Zurich. 1966. Louisville: Westminster/John Knox Press, 1991.

Bevan, Edwyn. *Symbolism and Belief*. 1938. Boston: Beacon Press, 1957.

Bitzer, Lloyd F. "The Rhetorical Situation." *Philosophy and Rhetoric*. I (1968): 1-14.

Boehme, Jacob. *The Way to Christ*. 1624. Trans. John Joseph Stoudt. New York: Harper & Brothers, 1947.

Booth, Wayne. *The Rhetoric of Fiction*. Chicago: University of Chicago Press, 1961.

_____. *Now Don't Try to Reason With Me*. Chicago: University of Chicago Press, 1970.

Bryant, Donald C. "Rhetoric: Its Function and Scope." *The Quarterly Journal of Speech* 39 (1953): 425.

Burke, Kenneth. "Literature as Equipment for Living." In *The Philosophy of Literary Form: Studies in Symbolic Action*. New York: 1957.

Carpenter, Humphrey. *Tolkien: A Biography*. New York: Ballantine Books, 1978.

Chesterton, G.K. *The Everlasting Man*. New York: Dodd, Mead & Company, 1925.

Como, James. "Elitism at the Core: Dare We Call it Rhetoric?" In *The Core and the Canon: A National Debate*. Eds. L. Robert Stevens, G. L. Seligmann, and Julian Long. Denton: University of North Texas Press, 1993.

Davidman, Joy. *Smoke on the Mountain: An Interpretation of the Ten Commandments*. Philadelphia: The Westminster Press, 1953.

Davies, Robertson. *The Deptford Trilogy*. New York: Penguin Books, 1990.

Dorsett, Lyle W. *And God Came In*. New York: Ballantine Books, 1983.

Easton, Stewart C. *Man and World in the Light of Anthroposophy*. Hudson: Anthroposophic Press, 1989.

Eddison, E. R. *The Worm Ouroboros*. 1926. New York: Ballantine Books, 1962.

Erickson, Carolly. *The Medieval Vision: Essays in History and Perception*. New York: Oxford University Press, 1976.

Examination Statutes (*Statt. Univ. Oxon. Tit. VI* and parts of *Tit. II, V, VIII* and *XII*) Academical Year 1920-21, Oxford: Clarendon Press, 1920.

Glyn, Patrick. *God: The Evidence*. Rocklin, Calif.: Prima, 1997.

Grahame, Kenneth. *The Wind in the Willows*. 1908. New York: St. Martin's Griffin, 1996.

Grant, Judith Skelton. *Robertson Davies, Man of Myth*. New York: Viking Press, 1994.

Griffiths, Dom Bede. *The Golden String*. Springfield, Ill.: Templegate Publishers, 1980.

Harris, Maxine. *The Loss That Is Forever.* New York: Penguin Books, 1996.

Harrison, Gilbert A. *The Enthusiast: A Life of Thornton Wilder.* New Haven: Ticknor & Fields, 1983.

Harwood, A. C. *The Voice of Cecil Harwood: A Miscellany.* Ed. Owen Barfield. London: Rudolph Steiner Press, 1979.

Higgins, James E. *Beyond Words: Mystical Fancy in Children's Literature.* New York: Teachers College Press, 1970.

Hirsch, E. D. *Validity in Interpretation.* New Haven: 1967.

Huizinga, Johan. *The Autumn of the Middle Ages.* Trans. Rodney J. Payton and Ulrich Mammitzsch. Chicago: University of Chicago Press, 1996.

John Paul II, Pope. *Crossing the Threshold of Hope.* Ed. Vittorio Messori. New York: Alfred A. Knopf, 1994.

_____. *The Gospel of Life.* New York: Times Books (Random House), 1995.

_____. *The Place Within: The Poetry of Pope John Paul II.* Trans. Jerzy Kiewicz. New York: Random House, 1982.

Joseph, H. W. B. *An Introduction to Logic.* Oxford: Oxford University Press, 1916.

Julian of Norwich. *Revelations of Divine Love.* Trans. Clifton Wolters. Hamondsworth: Penguin Books, 1966.

Lasch, Christopher. *The Culture of Narcissism: American Life in An Age of Diminishing Expectations.* New York: W. W. Norton & Co., 1978.

Law, William. *A Serious Call to a Devout and Holy Life* (1728) and *The Spirit of Love.* Ed. Paul G. Stanwood. The Classics of Western Spirituality. New York: Paulist Press, 1978.

Keegan, John. *The Face of Battle.* New York: Barnes & Noble Books, 1993.

Lindsay, David. *A Voyage to Arcturus.* 1920. London: Victor Gollancz Ltd., 1968.

MacDonald, George. *An Anthology.* Ed. C. S. Lewis. New York: Macmillan, 1947.

_____. *Diary of an Old Soul.* Minneapolis: Augsburg Publishing House, 1975.

_____. "The Imagination: Its Function and Its Culture," *A Dish of Orts.* London: Edwin Dalton, 1908.

_____. *Phantastes* (1858) and *Lilith* (1895). With an Introduction by C. S. Lewis. Grand Rapids: Wm. B. Eerdmans, 1964.

MacIntyre, Alasdair. *After Virtue.* Notre Dame: The University of Notre Dame Press, 1981.

McKenna, Stephen. *The Confessions of a Well-Meaning Woman.* London: Cassell and Company, 1922.

Menninger, Karl, M.D. *Whatever Became of Sin?* New York: Hawthorn Books, 1973.

Morris, William. *The Well at the World's End.* Phoenix Mill: Alan Sutton Publishing Limited, 1996.

Murphy, James J. "St. Augustine and the Debate About a Christian Rhetoric." *Quarterly Journal of Speech* 46 (1960): 400-10.

Newman, John Henry. *An Essay in Aid of a Grammar of Assent.* 1870; 8th ed. 1889. Ed. I. T. Ker. Oxford: Clarendon Press, 1985.

Otto, Rudolph. *The Idea of the Holy: An Inquiry into the non-rational factor in the idea of the divine and its relation to the rational.* 1917. Trans. John W. Harvey. 2nd ed. New York: Oxford University Press, 1958.

Percy, Walker. *The Message in the Bottle: How Queer Man Is, How Queer Language Is, and What One Has to Do with the Other.* New York: Farrar, Straus and Giroux, 1954.

_____. *The Second Coming.* New York: Farrar, Straus & Giroux, 1980.

_____. *Signposts in a Strange Land.* Ed. Patrick Samway. New York: Farrar, Straus and Giroux, 1991.

_____. *The Thanatos Syndrome.* New York: Farrar, Straus & Giroux, 1987.

Potter, Beatrix. *The Great Big Treasury of Beatrix Potter.* New York: Derrydale Books, 1992.

Raphael, Beverly. "The Young Child and the Death of a Parent." In *The Place of Attachment and Human Behavior*. Ed. Colin Murray Parkes and Joan Stevenson-Hinde. New York: Basic Books, 131-150.

Richards, I. A. *Principles of Literary Criticism*. London: Kegan Paul, Trench,Trubner, & Co., 1930.

_____. *Practical Criticism*. New York: 1929.

Sahler, Olle Jane Z., ed. *The Child and Death*. St. Louis: The C. V. Mosby Co., 1978.

Sayers, Dorothy L. *Creed or Chaos?* 1949. Manchester: Sophia Institute Press, 1974.

St. Francis de Sales. *Introduction to the Devout Life*. Trans. and ed. John K. Ryan. Garden City: Image Books (Doubleday and Company), 1972.

_____. *Thy Will Be Done: Letters to Persons in the World*. Trans. the Very Rev. Henry Benedict Mackey. Manchester: Sophia Institute Press, 1995.

St. Therese of Lisieux. *The Story of a Soul: The Autobiography of Therese of Lisieux*. 1898. Trans. John Beevers. Garden City: Image Books (Doubleday and Company), 1957.

Stephens, James. *The Crock of Gold*. 1912. New York: Macmillan, 1926.

Thonssen, Lester, A. Craig Baird, and Waldo W. Braden. *Speech Criticism*, 2nd ed. New York: 1970.

Todorov, Tzvetan. *The Fantastic: A Structural Approach to a Literary Genre*. Ithaca: Cornell Unviersity Press, 1973.

Tolson, Jay. *Pilgrim in the Ruins: A Life of Walker Percy*. New York: Simon & Schuster, 1992.

Toulmin, Stephen. *The Uses of Argument*. Cambridge: Cambridge University Press, 1958.

Vitz, Paul C. *Psychology as Religion: The Cult of Self-worship*. Grand Rapids: Wm. B. Eerdmans, 1977.

Webster, Richard. *Why Freud Was Wrong: Sin, Science, and Psychoanalysis*. New York: Basic Books, 1995.

Wilder, Thornton. *The Bridge of San Luis Rey.* New York: Albert & Charles Boni, 1928.

_____. *The Eighth Day.* New York: Harper & Row, 1967.

Williams, Charles. *The Place of the Lion.* New York: Pellegrini & Cudahy, 1951.

_____ and C. S. Lewis. *Taliessin Through Logres, The Region of the Summer Stars, Arthurian Torso.* Grand Rapids: Wm. B. Eerdmans, 1974.

Wilson, James Q. *The Moral Sense.* New York: The Free Press, 1993.

Winslow, Ola E., ed. *Jonathan Edwards: Basic Writings.* New York: 1966.

Index

Adams, Fr. Walter, 106.
Aeschliman, Michael D., 168.
Aldiss, Brian, 11.
Alexander, Samuel (*Space, Time and Deity*), 61, 78-79, 85, 162.
Anderson, Walter Truett, 3.
Anscombe, Elizabeth, 59, 172-73.
Anstey, F., 70.
anthroposophy, 29, 45, 80, 122.
apologetics, 12-14, 147.
Arianism and Arius, 14.
Aristotle, 142, 176; *Rhetoric*, 142-44.
Askins, William James ("Doc"), 45.

Baker, Leo, 33.
Barfield, Owen, 23, 29, 32, 38, 45, 80-81, 114, 179, 181, 198.

Barley, John, 59.
Barth, Karl (*Homiletics*), 147.
Baxter, Richard, 6, 15; *Church-History of the Government of Bishops* (as a source of "mere Christianity"), 88; *The Saint's Everlasting Rest*, 167.
Bayley, Peter, 199-200.
BBC, the, 7, 8, 29, 57.
Berkeley, Bishop George, 28, 76, 85.
Beversluis, John (*C. S. Lewis and the Search for Rational Religion*), 173-74, 188, 190.
Bevan, Edwyn, *Symbolism and Belief*, 68, 137.
Bide, Fr. Peter, 105.
Bloom, Harold, 11.
Boehme, Jacob, 61, 86; *Signatura Rerum* and *The Way of Christ*, 86-87.

Boorstin, Daniel, 10.
Booth, Wayne, 12-14.
Boss, Edgar, 60.
Brown, Sir Thomas (*Religio Medici*), 189.
Bryant, Donald C., 142.
Bultitude (the Whipsnade Zoo bear), 133.
Bulwer-Lytton, Edward, xi.
Bunyan, John, 6, 15, 48.
Burke, Kenneth, 189.
Bush, Douglas, 11.
Bush, George, 8.
Butler, Joseph, 88.

Calabria, Fr. Giovanni, 191-93.
Caroll, Lewis, 11.
Carritt, E. F., 28.
Carter, Stephen, 11.
Chesterton, G. K., 6, 12, 48, 61, 100, 107, 136; *The Everlasting Man*, 46, 57, 62-63.
Cicero, a bore, 27.
Coghill, Nevill, 27-28, 68, 117, 186.
constellations, of related writers and thinkers, 6, 11, 12, 33, 189.
Cooke, Alistair, 58.
Cox, John D., 137.
Crispin, Edmund, 174.

Dante, 15, 48.
Davies, Robertson, 8, 189.
Derrick, Christopher, 42

Dundas-Grant, James, 200.

early parental loss, 38-39.
Eddison, E. R. (*The Worm Ouroboros*), 66.
Edwards, Jonathan, 163.
Emerson, Ralph Waldo, 87.
Empson, William, 11; on Lewis, 6.
Erickson, Carolly (*The Medieval Vision*), 134.
existentialism, 100-01, 189-91, 197.

Farrer, Austin, 14, 24, 68, 147.
Fish, Stanley, 11.
Foligno, Angela de, 134.

genius, xi, 11; Lewis on, xi.
Gibb, Jocelyn, 23, 31.
Glyn, Patrick (*God: The Evidence*), 6.
Grahame, Kenneth, 61, 70, 135; *The Wind in the Willows*, 67-68, 132.
Green, Roger Lancelyn, 31-32.
Greeves, Arthur, 25-26, 43, 77-78, 198-99.
Griffiths, Dom Bede (*The Golden String*), xi, 104.

Haggard, H. Rider, 33.
Hamilton, Thomas, 35.

Hart, Dabney, 60.
Hart, Jeffrey, 71, 117.
Havard, Dr. R. E., 200.
Head, the Rev. R. E., 56.
Herbert, George (*Sketches of a Parson*), 89.
Hewetson, Fr. Christopher, Vicar, Holy Trinity Church, Headington Quarry, 9.
Higgins, James (*Beyond Words*), 130-31.
Holbrook, David, 59.
Holmer, Paul (*C.S. Lewis: The Shape of His Faith and Thought*), 136, 141-42, 190.
homiletics, 147-48
Horne, Brian, 68.
Hooker, Richard, 6, 15, 48, 62; *The Laws of Ecclesiastical Polity*, 64-66.
Hooper, Walter (*C. S. Lewis: Companion and Guide*), xiii, 9, 17, 168.
Huizinga, Johan, 100.
Hume, David, 28, 76, 154.

imagination, 29, 122-26, 132-33, 135.
Inklings, the, 32-33.

Jenkin, A. K. Hamilton, 78.
Johari Window, 54, 95.
John Paul II, Pope (*Crossing the Threshold of Hope*), 19, 105.

Johnson, Dr. Samuel, xi, 6, 7, 15, 60, 88.
Joseph, H. W. B. (*Introduction to Logic*), 27, 173.
Julian of Norwich, Lady, 97.

Kant, Immanuel, 28, 75.
Kazin, Alfred, 71.
Keegan, John (*The Face of Battle*), 41.
a Kempis, Thomas, (*The Imitation of Christ*), 91-92, 94, 106.
Kennedy, George A., 144.
Kierkegaard, Sören, 190.
Kilby, Clyde, 49, 60..
Kirkpatrick, W. T. ("The Great Knock"), 24-25, 26, 28, 39-40, 52, 84.
Kreeft, Peter, 176.

Ladborough, R. W., 32.64.
Lasch, Christopher (*The Culture of Narcissism*), 175.
Law, William, 6, 14, 70; *A Serious Call to a Devout and Holy Life*, 64, 87-88.
Lawlor, John, 31.
Leavis, F. R., 58, 72.
L'Engle, Madeleine, 170.
Lewis, Albert, 24-25, 35, 37, 39, 40, 46, 50-52, 87, 107, 114, 189.
LEWIS, C. S.: achievement, x, 5-7, 11-12, 175; as apologist,

x, xii, 5-6, 13, 17, 53, 121 149-
51, 157-60, 164-66, 198;
argumentativeness, 27-32,
39-40, 115, 116, 118, 139;
conversion, 34, 52, 75, 81, 83-
85, 99; commentators,
critics, and criticism, 57-60,
73, 117, 172-74; dreams, 45;
early parental loss, 39, 53,
181, 186, 193-94; the "Great
War," 29, 85; himself as an
example, 17, 19, 114, 181, 186;
home, 66, 77-78, 198-200;
influences (of and on), 8, 11,
60-70, 84-100; Irishness, 34-
35; Joy (*Sehnsucht*), 36, 41,
66, 75-77, 90, 130, 135, 162;
Little Lea, 25, 36; lust, 43-
44; medievalism, 85, 99-100,
134, 136-37; mere Christianity, 15, 18, 88; mother's
death, 37-38, 107, 181, 186-
88; "nominal" Christianity,
35; Protestantism, 71, 96,
120; provident voice of, 5;
psychological divides and
spiritual confusion, 41-42,
45-47, 53, 75, 95, 101, 112-13,
178-79, 194, 199; reputation,
ix-x, 7-10, 57; rhetoric, 140,
145-47, 167-68, 175-79, 180-
81, 196-98; sacramentalism,
128-30, 132, 134-38; the self
(with introspection), 23-24,
54, 56-57, 70, 76, 79-81, 83,
85-86, 95-99, 106, 108, 114,
116, 118-19, 131, 173, 178-81,

184-85, 188, 191-94, 197;
Socratic Club, 59; stature, x;
talkativeness, 23-24, 111-12;
Time cover, 8; theatricality,
30; *topoi*, 167-71; veiled
genres, 181-88; vocation, 24,
84, 103, 141; *weiberherr-
schaft*, 42, 46; will, 23, 53-54,
84, 94; works of mercy, 101-
05; World War I, 41, 53, 107.
Works: *Abolition of Man*, 12,
65, 120; *The Allegory of
Love*, 117, 128; *All My Road
Before Me: The Diary of C.S.
Lewis, 1922-1927*, 44-46, 198;
Animal Land, 25; "The
Anthropological Approach,"
117; "The Apologist's
Evening Prayer," 179; "As the
Ruin Falls," 178; "Bluspels
and Flalansferes," 121-23;
Broadcast Talks, 57; *The
Case for Christianity*, 58;
"Christian Apologetics," 15,
159-60; *Christian
Reflections*, 195; *The
Chronicles of Narnia*, 8, 11,
57, 129-38, 180, 199; "On
Criticism," 60; "Dangers of
National Repentance," 115;
The Dark Tower, 69; "*De
Descriptione Temporum*,"
112-13; "Delinquents in the
Snow," 172; "Democratic
Education," 115; *The
Discarded Image*, 99-100,
177; *Dymer*, 46-49, 52, 72;

"The Efficacy of Prayer," 104
148; *English Literature in the
Sixteenth-Century, Exclud-
ing Drama,* 57, 96, 102, 105,
146; *An Experiment in
Criticism,* 16, 55, 120, 124; ;
"On Forgiveness," 191;
Forms of Things Unknown,
184; *The Four Loves,* 57, 107,
181, 183; "The Genesis of a
Medieval Book," 60; *George
MacDonald: An Anthology,*
93-97; *God in the Dock,* 159;
The Great Divorce, 64, 70,
93, 135, 152, 177, 183, 184; *A
Grief Observed,* 116, 174, 181,
185-86, 188, 197; "The
Humanitarian Theory of
Punishment," 115; *Is
Theology Poetry?,"* 137; *The
Last Battle,* 130, 131, 183;
"Learning in War-Time,"
148; "Legion," 95; *Letters to
an American Lady,* 180;
Letters to Malcolm, 64, 68,
92, 99, 104, 105, 162-64, 181-
83, 189; *The Lion, the Witch
and the Wardrobe,* 193; "On
Living in the Atomic Age,"
19; "The Literary Impact of
the Authorized Version," 60;
The Magician's Nephew, 8,
129, 133, 181, 186-88; "The
Man Born Blind," 138; "Man
or Rabbit," 18; "Meditation
in a Toolshed," 160-62; *Mere
Christianity,* 7, 8, 24, 54, 156,

158, 172, 174, 178; *Miracles,*
59, 63, 125-26, 153-56, 158,
183, 186; "Modern Man and
His Categories of Thought,"
18; "Myth Became Fact," 124;
"The Necessity of Chivalry,"
115; "Obstinacy in Belief,"
174; *Out of the Silent Planet,*
69, 112, 121, 180; *Perelandra,*
69, 121, 125-28 152, 153-56,
184; *The Personal Heresy,*
117-19, 181; "Petitionary
Prayer: A Problem without
an Answer," 104; *The
Pilgrim's Regress,* 70, 72-75,
112, 124, 128, 141, 180, 181;
"The Poison of Subjectiv-
ism," 5, 115; *A Preface to
'Paradise Lost',* 117, 146; *The
Prince Caspian,* 136; *The
Problem of Pain,* 8, 53, 107,
153-56; "Psychoanalysis and
Literary Criticism," 117; *The
Queen of Drum,* 177
"Reason," 151; *Reflections on
the Psalms,* 57, 63, 107, 129,
181-82; "Religion and
Rocketry," 116; "Shelley,
Dryden, and Mr. Eliot," 124;
The Screwtape Letters, 7, 8,
11, 57, 68, 70, 139, 165-66;
"The Seeing Eye," 116, 195;
"Sex in Literature," 115; *The
Silver Chair,* 129, 135, 137,
156-57, 177, 189; *Spirits in
Bondage,* 7; *Surprised by Joy,*
25 and *passim,* 57, 73, 100,

176, 181-82; *That Hideous Strength*, 73, 112, 121; *Till We Have Faces*, 11, 57, 68, 70, 152, 177, 181, 183-85; "Three Kinds of Men," 189; "Transposition," 148; "The Trouble with 'X' . . . ," 18, 91; "Two Ways with the Self," 97; *The Voyage of the 'Dawn Treader'*, 90, 132; "We Have No 'Right to Happiness'," 106; "The Weight of Glory," 148.

Lewis, Flora (Florence Augusta), 35-37, 51, 194.

Lewis, Joy Davidman, 31, 53, 104, 105, 150, 171, 178, 186, 188, 191, 194, 197.

Lewis, Warren Hamilton, 25, 32-33, 35, 40, 49-50, 87, 107, 197; Lewis Family Papers, 49; *Brothers & Friends*, 4, 50, 52.

Lindsay, David, 61, 68, 70; *A Voyage to Arcuturus*, 69-70.

Lobdell, Jared C., 60.

Lock, John, 28.

Lorenz, Conrad (*King Solomon's Ring*), 133.

Lunn, Sir Arnold, 12.

Luther, Martin, 188, 198.

MacDonald, Dwight, 11.

MacDonald, George, 6, 12, 61, 70, 85, 93-99, 102, 107, 130, 135 (*A Dish of Orts*); *Phantastes*, 26, 48.

MacIntyre, Alasdair (*After Virtue*), 175.

Martlets, the, 27.

Mead, Marjorie, 49.

Meilaender, Gilbert, 168.

Mission and Ministry, 4.

Mathew, Fr. Gervase, 111.

Menninger, Dr. Karl (*Whatever Became of Sin?*), 175.

Modern Language Association, 10.

Moore, Mr. Courtenay Edward, 40.

Moore, Mrs. Janie King ("Minto"), 40, 42, 45-51, 102, 107, 188, 192-94.

Moore, Maureen, 40, 42.

Moore, Paddy (Edward Frances Courtenay), 40-42, 197.

Morris, William, 27, 44; *The Well at the World's End*, 66.

Mr. Papworth (Lewis's dog), 132.

Myers, Doris T., 123.

Nesbitt, E., 61, 67, 70.

Neuhaus, Fr. Richard John, 11.

New Catholic Encyclopedia, The, 147.

Newman, John Henry, Cardinal and the Illative Sense, (*An Essay in Aid of a Grammar of Assent*), 196.

New York C. S. Lewis Society, the, 121.

This book was designed and set into type
by Mitchell S. Muncy,
with cover art by Stephen J. Ott,
and printed and bound
by Quebecor Printing Book Press
Brattleboro, Vermont.

The text face is Minion,
designed by Robert Slimbach
and issued in digital form by Adobe Systems,
Mountain View, California, in 1991.

The paper is acid-free and is of archival quality.

11